experienc

al responsibility to pass

are the nursery of

nust share them too;

e and distort our

g after us will be con-

We cannot afford

g it up to historians to

r fifty or one hundred

ent conditions demand

tories now."

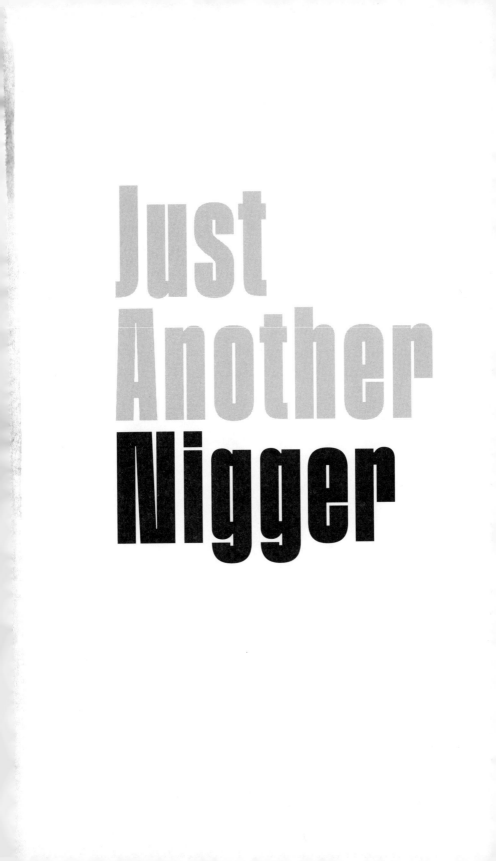

Just Another Nigger

Just Another Nigger

or

Use What You Got to Get What You Need

Don Cox

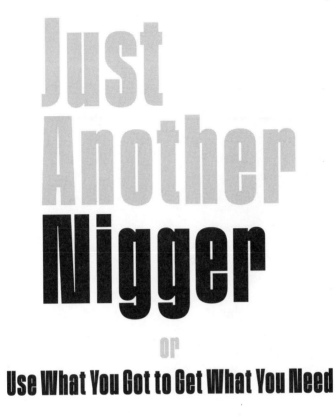

Foreword by Kimberly Cox Marshall

Introduction by Steve Wasserman

HEYDAY, BERKELEY, CALIFORNIA

Library of Congress Cataloging-in-Publication Data

Names: Cox, Donald, 1936-2011, author.
Title: Just another nigger : my life in the Black Panther Party or use what you got to get what you need / Don Cox.
Description: Berkeley, California : Heyday, [2018]
Identifiers: LCCN 2018004946| ISBN 9781597144599 (hardcover : alk. paper) | ISBN 9781597144605 (e-pub)
Subjects: LCSH: Cox, Donald, 1936-2011. | Black Panther Party--History. | African Americans--Missouri--Biography.
Classification: LCC E185.615 .C692 2018 | DDC 322.4/20973--dc23
LC record available at https://lccn.loc.gov/2018004946

Book and Cover Design by Ashley Ingram

Orders, inquiries, and correspondence should be addressed to:
Heyday
P.O. Box 9145, Berkeley, CA 94709
(510) 549-3564
www.heydaybooks.com

Printed in Dexter, Michigan, by Thomson-Shore

10 9 8 7 6 5 4 3 2 1

"In my own country for nearly a century
I have been nothing but a nigger."

—*W. E. B. Du Bois*

Contents

Foreword

Kimberly Cox Marshall

Promise made, promise kept. I didn't know that when he put his manuscript in my hands and made me promise to publish it after he passed, that would be the last time I saw him. But now it's done: promise made, promise kept. And, yes, Daddy, I kept the title you wanted.

My first memories of Daddy are of the time we spent with his family. It seemed like almost every weekend we were either at his sister Irene's or his aunt and uncle's in Mountain View, about forty miles south of San Francisco, where we lived. His two sisters that lived out here in California, Irene and Mary Jane, doted on their younger brother, and that affection trickled down to me. How I loved my aunts! When I would visit, they would always have grapes with the skin peeled off, because "Donald's daughter didn't like the skin." Every year until she couldn't, my Aunt Irene sent me two dollars, and then five dollars (for inflation, as she said) for my Birthday Ice-Cream Cone. They were like that until they passed.

And then there was Daddy himself.

I have so many good memories of us together. I remember him picking me up from the San Francisco School of Ballet, and there he would be in his Austin-Healey, always with the top down. He would drive through Golden Gate Park so I could sit in the back and throw kisses like I was Miss America. When I would say I was going to hang out on the beach, like I saw girls doing in the movies, he never said anything to stop me. I realize now that I was never going to be in the San Francisco production of *The Nutcracker,* I wasn't going to be Miss America, and most beaches had signs to keep me and my kind out, but Daddy never told me I couldn't do any of those things. For him, I had no limitations.

I also loved our weekend outings to the movies as I got older and he started getting political. I didn't recognize it then, but I do now: all of the movies were war movies. And as it turned out, watching all those tactical storylines paid off for me, and for him. I remember one time, during the years Daddy was in the Black Panther Party and I was going to private school in the Richmond District of San Francisco, there was a man known for accosting and molesting young girls in the area. That same man had followed me to school one day, and as soon as I was inside the building I called my family to tell them about it. A week later, as I was getting off the bus, there was Daddy waiting at my stop, dressed in his old Brooks Brothers suit and with his afro cut off. He gave me a look that said I should be quiet and opened his jacket to show me he was carrying. I got off the bus and went on ahead to walk the five blocks to school, and although Daddy was nowhere to be seen, I knew he was watching my every move.

Another time, when I was going to a Lutheran school, I wore my hair in a curly afro one day. How proud I was—until I got to school. The principal told me my hair looked a mess. I promptly called Daddy, and I don't remember what I told him, but the next thing I knew, here comes Daddy and about four or five Panthers looking fine and sharp in all-black turtlenecks, pants, leather coats, and berets. I never heard my Daddy raise his voice—I think I would have crapped in my pants if I did—and when he spoke, he always spoke eloquently and softly and looked you directly in the eyes. For people who didn't know him, that alone could make them crap in their pants. I didn't hear what he said to the principal that day, but at the end of the year I left that school for good.

When I was ten or twelve years old, we lived down the hill from Alamo Square, and whenever I heard the helicopters, I would ride my bike looking for friends to come with me to the Panther office. We would ride to the top of the square to see if there were more than two "eyes in the sky" (helicopters), and if so we would ride our bikes to the Panther office—us dumb kids figuring the cops wouldn't shoot if there were kids around.

Here are some things I learned from Daddy:

My family taught me empathy, and Daddy was never one to shy away from showing it.

I loved marching with him in the CORE (Congress of Racial Equality) protest marches of the early sixties, and even though I was probably too young for it, I was exposed to many important things there.

During events put on for the fiftieth anniversary of the founding of the Black Panther Party, in 2016, I had men search me out to tell me that if it wasn't for Daddy they don't know where they would have ended up in life—that he taught them so much.

He and my mother also taught me we have to invest in our young people, as they are our future.

Among all the things I'm grateful for, one thing that stands out is this: I got to meet Stokely Carmichael (later, Kwame Ture) and his wife, Miriam Makeba, when they came to dinner at my grandparents' house. I didn't realize it at the time (but I so cherish the memory now) that I was being taught about apartheid literally at the knee of "Mama Africa." I remember she told me a story of how her brother wasn't legally allowed to ride his bike at night in their native South Africa because they had to come indoors when it got dark. I was about twelve at the time and could hardly believe my ears, such a story was so foreign to my experience. I always remember that conversation because everyone around me got so quiet. I can imagine where those memories took my grandparents and great-grandmother, who were from the South.

No matter how proud I was of Daddy's activities, though, there was also a flipside. Schoolmates stopped playing with me and inviting me to their parties because of Daddy's politics. A relative that had the same last name changed it for a time so they would not be associated with our family. Our phone was tapped. The eye in the sky would flash its spotlight into my bedroom window, and sometimes we would come home and find the FBI surrounding the house or Daddy's car—the GTO he drove to Nevada to buy guns. My mother would literally shoo the police away like flies. I heard once Daddy had even used a dead baby's death certificate to get a fake passport. When things started to go bad in the party, there were two kidnapping attempts on me, and one night a woman came to our house to kill my mother, brother, and me. We can only thank goodness that she was so high she couldn't go through with it. My mother talked her down and she left. By then things were so bad that Daddy left the United States and started his life in exile. I would not see him for thirteen years, and I communicated with him only about five times before I saw him again in 1984.

By then I had become a woman, gotten married, had a child, and divorced. When I saw him again in Paris, I wasn't that wide-eyed girl anymore. I had taken off the rose-colored glasses and realized that Daddy was just a man, faults and all. I was taken aback to learn that even though he had married a wonderful woman after divorcing my mother, he still saw the need to have a mistress, whom he wanted me to meet. I assumed this was the French way at the time, but I was American, and anyway, if it wasn't wrong, why did he ask me to keep it quiet? I mention this now because it was one of the things he despised about his own father—that his father would give money to his mistress to give to the church but wouldn't give money to his own mother. It was also eye-opening to read his manuscript and see how he treated women when he himself had a daughter who he was raising to have the views I have. These are things I wish we could have talked about.

As you read this book, you will realize that this man was like two sides of a coin. At the forty-fifth anniversary of the Black Panther Party, a close comrade confessed that he didn't know my father even had kids (myself and two brothers) until he read his obituary. It seems he had some success keeping his family away from the party, but, although he tried, he couldn't completely keep the party away from his family. As I grew up the daughter of Donald Cox, the Panthers and their dramas were never far away.

Introduction

Steve Wasserman

More than fifty years ago, in October 1966, back in what seems at this remove the Pleistocene era, Huey P. Newton and Bobby Seale, brash upstarts from Oakland, California, founded the Black Panther Party for Self-Defense. They quickly garnered a reputation for their willingness to stand up to police harassment and worse. They made a practice of shadowing the cops, California Penal Code in one hand, twelve-gauge shotgun in the other. Soon they were holding street-corner rallies and confronting officials, arguing that only by taking up arms could the black community put a stop to police brutality. Newton and Seale were fearless and cocky—even reckless, some felt—and itching for a fight.

Don Cox, thirty-two years old, married with two young children, and working in San Francisco as a commercial photographer, had participated in numerous Bay Area civil rights protests, but, over time, his discontent with the slow pace of change had deepened while his desire for more militant action mounted. He greatly admired how Newton "practiced what he preached," how "with gun in hand he faced down armed, racist policemen," how the Panthers were "ready to kill." Born in Missouri, Cox was proud of his rebel lineage. According to family lore, his grandfather, Joseph A. Cox, rode with Jesse James and was well known for his independent streak, which included marrying a young Swiss immigrant,

Maria Müller, at a time when interracial marriage risked not just racist condemnation and social ostracism but even lynching. The family was no stranger to guns, and young Don Cox gained a deserved reputation as something of a sharpshooter.

Alarmed by the Panthers' growing prominence, in 1967 California legislator Donald Mulford introduced a bill to ban the carrying of loaded weapons in public. Newton responded by upping the ante, and in early May of that year he dispatched thirty Panthers, most of them armed, to Sacramento. They showed up at the state capitol building as the bill was being debated. The police confiscated their guns soon after they arrived, but later returned them, as the Panthers had broken no laws. The Mulford Act passed, but the Panthers became instantly notorious, with images of their armed foray splashed across the nation's newspapers and shown on television. It was a PR coup. Soon thousands of black Americans joined the party, among them Don Cox. By the end of 1968, seventeen Panther chapters had opened across the country. One enthusiast quoted in a major feature story in the *New York Times Magazine* spoke for many, including Cox, when he said: "As far as I'm concerned it's beautiful that we finally got an organization that don't walk around singing. I'm not for all this talking stuff. When things start happening I'll be ready to die if that's necessary and it's important that we have somebody around to organize us."

The rise and fall of the Black Panther Party is a heartbreaking saga of heroism and hubris that, in its full dimension and contradiction, has long awaited its ideal chronicler. The material is rich, some of it still radioactive. A good deal of it can be found in the clutch of memoirs by ex-Panthers—inevitably self-serving but valuable nonetheless—that have appeared sporadically over the years, including those by Bobby Seale, David Hilliard, and Elaine Brown, and lesser-known figures such as William Lee Brent, Flores Forbes, and Jamal Joseph, and in books and articles by non-Panthers, especially those by David Horowitz, Kate Coleman, Hugh Pearson, and by sociologist Joshua Bloom and historian Waldo E. Martin, Jr., whose *Black Against Empire* is a flawed but indispensable history of the party. All are to be read with care.

To this literature we may now add Don Cox's revelatory, even incendiary story of his five years in the Black Panther Party, from his work as Field Marshal in charge of weapons procurement, gunrunning, and planning armed attacks and defense—including tales told for the first time in this memoir—to his star turn as a party spokesman raising money at the Manhattan home of Leonard Bernstein and his wife, Felicia, for which he was famously mocked by writer Tom Wolfe, to his eventual flight to Algeria to join Panther leader Eldridge Cleaver, to his decision to leave the party in 1972, following his disillusionment with Newton's leadership. Cox would live out the rest of his life in self-imposed exile in France, in the mountain village of Camps-sur-l'Agly, where he wrote these unrepentant recollections in the early eighties, enjoining his daughter, Kimberly, to promise him she would do everything she could to have them published after his death. Cox died in 2011 at age seventy-four.

The Panthers were controversial in their day and remain so. Peopled by outsize characters—starting with magnetic and headstrong founder Huey P. Newton, eulogized at his 1989 funeral as "our Moses"—the party's complicated history, replete with Byzantine political schisms, murderous infighting, and a contested legacy, has eluded sober examination. Its story is swaddled in propaganda, some of it promulgated by enemies who sought assiduously to destroy it, and some spread by apologists and hagiographers who lionized the party's admirable efforts to bring education, food, clothing, and medical treatment into America's impoverished ghettos while refusing to acknowledge the party's crimes and misdemeanors, preferring to attribute its demise almost entirely to the machinations of others. Cox is not among them. His memoir is notable for his unsentimental and, by turns, self-critical approach.

One of the things that attracted Cox and others to the Black Panther Party was its refusal to go along with the narrow cultural nationalism that appealed to many African Americans at that time. The party's dispute with Ron Karenga's US Organization, for example, was rooted in this profound disagreement. The Panthers fought tremendous battles, some turning deadly, with those who thought, as the saying went, that political power grew out of the sleeve of a dashiki. By contrast, the Panthers embraced a class-based politics with an internationalist bent. Inspired by anti-imperialist struggles in Africa, Latin America, and Asia, they began by emphasizing local issues but soon went global, ultimately establishing, as Cox vividly recounts, an International Section in Algiers. Their romance with the liberation movements of others would eventually become something of a fetish, reaching its nadir in the bizarre adulation of North Korea's dictator Kim Il-sung and his watchword *Juche*, a term for the self-reliance that the Panthers deluded themselves into thinking might be the cornerstone of a revolutionary approach that would find an echo of enthusiasm in America.

In the beginning, little about the party was original. Even the iconic dress of black leather jackets and matching berets was inspired by earlier Oakland activists, such as the now-all-but-forgotten Mark Comfort. As early as February 1965, the month Malcolm X was assassinated, Comfort had launched a protest to "put a stop to police beating innocent people." Later that summer, Comfort and his supporters demanded that the Oakland City Council "keep white policemen out of black neighborhoods" and together took steps to organize citizen patrols to "monitor the actions of the police and document incidents of brutality."

This wasn't enough for Newton and Seale. Inspired by Robert F. Williams's advocacy and practice of "armed self-reliance"—for which he'd had to flee the country in the early 1960s, seeking sanctuary in Castro's Cuba—Newton and Seale decided to break entirely with "armchair intellectualizing," as Seale would later call it. Propaganda of the deed, they believed, would arouse the admiration of, in Newton's words, the "brothers on the block." They'd had it with bended-knee politics. It was time, as a favored slogan of the party would later urge, to "pick up the gun." Drawing up a ten-point program with demands for justice and self-determination, the Panthers represented a rupture with the reformist activism of the traditional civil rights movement, and it wasn't long before the party saw itself as a vanguard capable of jump-starting a revolution. For some, including Don Cox, it was an intoxicating fever dream. I, too, was not exempt, and I hope I shall not exceed the bounds of readers' indulgence if I share my own stake in the story that Cox so ably tells.

In early November 1969, I left Berkeley for a few days and went to Chicago to support the Chicago Eight, then on trial for the bloody police riot that had marred the anti–Vietnam War protests at the 1968 Democratic National Convention. I knew some of the defendants: Jerry Rubin, organizer of one of the first teach-ins against the Vietnam War, whom I'd met four years before while organizing the first junior high school protest against the Vietnam War; Tom Hayden, a founder of Students for a Democratic Society (SDS) and principal author of *The Port Huron Statement*, who'd taken an interest in my rabble-rousing posse at Berkeley High School during the People's Park protest of May 1969; and Bobby Seale, whom I'd encountered through my close friendship with schoolmates who'd joined the Panthers, especially Ronald Stevenson, with whom I co-led a successful student strike in 1968 that established the first black studies and history department in an American public high school. It was Bobby who'd let a group of us use the party's typesetting machines in its Shattuck Avenue national headquarters to put together an underground newspaper, *Pack Rat.*

In the Chicago Eight trial, Seale had been bound and gagged in the courtroom—a "neon oven," activist and defendant Abbie Hoffman had called it—and the country was riveted by the appalling spectacle. I arrived at the apartment rented by Leonard Weinglass, one of the defense attorneys, who was using it as a crash pad and general meeting place for the far-flung tribe of supporters and radical nomads, unafraid to let their freak flags fly, who sought to muster support for the beleaguered defendants.

Sometime around midnight, Fred Hampton, leader of the Chicago chapter of the Black Panther Party, clad in a long black leather coat and looking for all the world like a gunslinger bursting into a saloon, swept in with a couple of other Panthers in tow. You could feel the barometric pressure in the room rise with their entrance. At the time, the favored flick was Sam Peckinpah's *The Wild Bunch*, an epic Western revenge fantasy that inflamed the overheated imaginations of a number of unindicted coconspirators like my friend Stew Albert, a founder of the Yippies. Hampton was already in the crosshairs of the FBI and Chicago mayor Richard Daley's goons, to whom he'd been a taunting nemesis. He had an open face, and his eyes flashed intelligently. He had the Panther swagger down pat, yet his voice was soft, welcoming. He radiated charisma and humility. He seemed tired, and somehow you knew he was already thinking of himself as a dead man walking. He was famous for having proclaimed, "You can kill a revolutionary, but you can't kill the revolution." You could see how people fell for him, and you could well imagine how his enemies hated and feared him. A month later he was murdered, betrayed by a paid undercover informant and shot dead by police while sleeping in his bed. He was twenty-one.

Hampton seemed destined for greatness, having already eclipsed in his seriousness Eldridge Cleaver, the party's minister of information and an ex-con who'd written the bestselling *Soul on Ice*. Cleaver was regarded by many of the younger recruits within the party as their Malcolm X. A strong advocate of working with progressive whites, Cleaver was a man of large appetites, an anarchic and ribald spirit who relished his outlaw status. After years in prison, he was hell-bent on making up for lost time and wasn't about to kowtow to anyone—not to Ronald Reagan, whom he mocked mercilessly, nor, as it would turn out, to Huey Newton. Like so many of the Panthers, he also had killer looks, inhabiting his own skin with enviable ease. (The erotic aura that the Panthers presented was a not inconsiderable part of their appeal, as any of the many photographs that were taken of them show. In this department, however, Huey was inarguably the Supreme Leader, and he never let you forget it.) Eldridge was the biggest mouth in a party of big mouths, and he especially loved invective and adored the sound of his own voice, delivered in a sly baritone drawl. He was the joker in the Panther deck and a hard act to follow. He was a gifted practitioner of the rhetoric of denunciation, favoring such gems as "fascist mafioso" and given to vilifying the United States at every turn as "Babylon." He was a master of misogynist pith, uttering the imperishable "revolutionary power grows out of the lips of a pussy," and he was fond of repeating, as if it were a personal mantra, "He could look his mama in the eye and lie." He was notorious in elite Bay Area movement circles for his many and persistent infidelities and for his physical abuse of his equally tough-talking and beautiful wife, Kathleen. About these failures, however, a curtain of silence was drawn. He was, all in all, a hustler who exuded charm and menace in equal measure, as Cox's memoir confirms. Cleaver would ultimately flee the country, rightly fearing a return to prison for parole violation following his bungled shootout with Oakland police in the immediate aftermath of the assassination of Martin Luther King, Jr., in April 1968. (Don Cox, who was ostensibly in charge of the party's clandestine military operations, apparently had little to do with Cleaver's abrupt and ill-conceived decision to ambush the officers.) The debacle had given the Panthers their first martyr, seventeen-year-old Bobby Hutton, the nascent party's first recruit, gunned down by the cops as he sought to surrender. His funeral was front-page news; Marlon Brando was a featured speaker. Cleaver was arrested, released on bail, and then disappeared, heading first to Cuba and then to Algeria, where Cox and other Panthers and sympathizers would later join him.

When Cleaver fled, Newton was still in prison, awaiting trial for killing an Oakland cop. Now Bobby Seale was fighting to avoid a similar fate in Chicago. David Hilliard, the party's chief of staff, was left to try to hold the group together. Hoover's FBI, sensing victory, ratcheted up its secret COINTELPRO campaign, in concert with local police departments across the country, to sow dissension in the party's ranks and to otherwise discredit and destroy its leaders. Hoover was a determined foe; he too had seemingly embraced Malcolm X's defiant slogan "By any means necessary." He cared a lot about order and about the law not a whit. With King gone, he worried, not unreasonably, that the Panthers would widen their appeal and step into the breach.

The suppression of the urban rebellions that erupted in many of the nation's cities in the hinge year of 1968 underscored the Panthers' fear that the United States had entered a long night of fascism. Nonviolent protest struck a growing number of activists as having run its course in the face of unsentimental and overwhelming state power. The Vietnam War, despite the upwelling of the Tet Offensive, seemed endless. Richard Nixon's election on a platform of "law and order" made a generation of reform-minded progressives seem hopelessly naïve. Fires were being lit by a burgeoning and increasingly despairing discontent. For some time, Jim Morrison had been singing of "The End." Soon, Gil Scott-Heron would intone that "The Revolution Will Not Be Televised," and from his California prison cell, Huey P. Newton began to dream of "revolutionary suicide."

The party began to crack under persistent government pressure, and internecine quarrels became ferocious and sometimes deadly. There were fierce clashes, large and small, over personalities and politics. Only later would the details emerge. For example, former Panther leader Elaine Brown gave a hair-raising account in her autobiography *A Taste of Power* (1992) of how Newton viciously turned on Seale, his comrade and peerless organizer (some details of which are disputed by

Seale). She recalled how Newton succumbed to his cocaine-and-cognac-fueled megalomania; how he ordered Big Bob Heard, his six-foot-eight, four-hundred-pound bodyguard, to beat Seale with a bullwhip, cracking twenty lashes across Bobby's bared back; how, when the ordeal was over, Newton abruptly stripped Seale of his rank as party chairman and ordered him to pack up and get out of Oakland. David Hilliard, too, Newton's friend since they were thirteen, would be expelled, as would his brother, June. Also ousted was Seale's brother, John, deemed by Newton to be "untrustworthy as a blood relative of a counterrevolutionary." Newton became what he arguably had been from the start: a sawdust Stalin. About this transformation Cox is remarkably forthcoming.

Still later, Flores Forbes, a trusted enforcer for Newton, came clean. He was a stalwart of the party's Orwellian "Board of Methods and Corrections," and a member of what Newton called his "Buddha Samurai," a praetorian guard made up of men willing to follow orders unquestioningly and do the "stern stuff." Forbes had joined the party at fifteen and wasted no time becoming a zombie for Huey. Forbes was bright and didn't have to be told; he knew when to keep his mouth shut. He well understood the "right to initiative," a term Forbes tells us "was derived from our reading and interpretation of *Wretched of the Earth* by Frantz Fanon." What Forbes took Fanon to mean was that "it is the oppressed people's right to believe that they should kill their oppressor in order to obtain their freedom. We just modified it somewhat to mean anyone who's in our way," like inconvenient witnesses who might testify against Newton, or Panthers who'd run afoul of Newton and needed to be "mud-holed"—battered and beaten to a bloody pulp. Newton no longer favored Mao's *Little Red Book*, preferring Mario Puzo's *The Godfather*, which he extolled for its protagonists' Machiavellian cunning and ruthlessness. Newton admired Melvin van Peebles's movie *Sweet Sweetback's Baadasssss Song,* the tale of a hustler who becomes a revolutionary. Military regalia was out, swagger sticks were in. Newton dropped the rank of minister of defense in favor of other titles. Some days he wanted to be called Supreme Commander, other days Servant of the People or, usually, just Servant. But to fully understand Huey's devolution, you'd have to run Peebles's picture backward, as the story of a revolutionary who becomes a hustler. To these horrors, Cox adds his own story of self-inflicted wounds revolving around the cult of personality and the murderous megalomania of his erstwhile comrades, including Eldridge Cleaver.

Some years ago, I spent an afternoon with Bobby Seale, renewing a conversation we'd begun months before. He'd moved back to Oakland, living once again in his mother's house, and was contemplating writing a book—the truth, the whole truth, and nothing but the truth, as he put it to me, about the rise and fall of the Panthers—on the very dining room table where almost a half century ago he and Newton had drafted the Panthers' Ten-Point Program. No one was getting any younger, and he felt he owed it to a new generation to speak frankly. At his invitation, we jumped into his car and, with Bobby at the wheel, drove around Oakland, visiting all the neighborhood spots where history had been made. Here was the corner where Newton had shot and killed Officer John Frey in October 1967; and there was the former lounge and bar, the notorious Lamp Post, where Newton had laundered money from drug deals and shakedowns; and over there were the steps of the Alameda County Courthouse, where thousands, including myself, had assembled in August 1970 to hail Newton's release from prison and where, beneath the blazing summer sun, Huey, basking in the embrace of the adoring crowd, had stripped off his shirt, revealing his cut and muscle-bound torso, honed by a punishing regimen of countless push-ups in the isolation cell of the prison where he'd done his time, a once slight Oakland kid now physically transformed into the very embodiment of the powerful animal he'd made the emblem of his ambitions.

As Seale spoke, mimicking with uncanny accuracy Huey's oddly high-pitched and breathless stutter, virtually channeling the man, now dead more than two decades—ignominiously gunned down at age forty-seven in a crack cocaine deal gone bad by a young punk half his age seeking to make his bones—it became clear that, despite everything he'd endured, Bobby Seale was a man with all the passions and unresolved resentments of a lover betrayed. There could be little doubt that, for Seale, the best years of his life were the years he'd spent devoted to Newton, who, despite the passage of time, still loomed large. Seale, like the party he gave birth to, couldn't rid himself of Huey's shadow.

Among the challenges in grappling with the Panthers and their legacy is keeping in reasonable and proportionate balance the multiple and often overlapping factors that combined to throttle the party. The temptation to overemphasize the role of the FBI is large. It should be avoided. There is no doubt about the evil that was done by Hoover's COINTELPRO: It exacerbated the worst tendencies among the Panthers and did much to deepen a politics of paranoia that would ultimately help hollow out what had been a steadily growing movement of opposition. It sowed the seeds of disunity. It cast doubt on the very idea of leadership. It promoted suspicion and distrust.

It countenanced murder and betrayal. But the Panthers themselves were not blameless. Newton, for his part, provided fertile ground for reckless extremism and outright criminality to grow and take root. Cockamamie offshoots like Donald DeFreeze's so-called Symbionese Liberation Army and even the lethal cult of Jim Jones's benighted Peoples Temple owed an unacknowledged debt to Newton's example. His responsibility for enfeebling his own and his party's best ambitions, gutting its achievements and compromising its ability to appeal to the unconvinced majority of his fellow citizens, is too often neglected in any number of books purporting to tell the party's story. Don Cox's memoir is an exception. It is precisely the sort of postmortem that is necessary for any proper and just understanding of the party's politics and history. It is a brave and honest book and a welcome contribution to a historical reckoning that is long overdue.

1

Joe Cox's Grandson

It was a cool dawn, April 14, 1936, when I tore my way into this world—feet first and weighing twelve pounds—my delivery further complicated by some difficulty in getting me to breathe. The umbilical cord, wrapped around my neck, was strangling me. Mine was a troubled introduction into life.

We lived on a small subsistence farm close to a village called Appleton City, Missouri, about eighty miles southeast of Kansas City. It supplied us with our vegetables, poultry, eggs, smoked pork, milk, and butter. Occasionally Mama sold some eggs or an extra pound or two of butter, but it wasn't anything systematic. In winter about one meal a week came from hunting.

I was preceded by one brother, Junior, and three sisters, Irene, Mary Jane, and Marleeta. Papa worked in town at the Ford garage as a mechanic. He had taken a correspondence course to learn the trade, and proudly displayed his huge framed diploma on the living room wall. He worked the land, slopped the hogs, and fed the cow in the morning and evening, before and after work and on weekends. Mama held down the house, the poultry, and the vegetable plot, plus cooked three meals a day and did the Monday washing. And every minute in between was spent sewing something—creating an article of clothing for someone in the family or making patchwork quilts, masterpieces worthy of any museum.

My memories begin during the Second World War, after

Pearl Harbor. Junior was away in Parsons, Kansas, doing public-works jobs at a Civilian Conservation Corps camp, and when he came home on leave in his sharp uniform, I assumed he was a special kind of a soldier. Irene was about two hours away in Sedalia, attending high school. I thought she was the most beautiful woman in the world; she was my standard of beauty. Mary Jane, the oldest at home, worked right alongside Mama, and Marleeta and I just played every day. Her year-and-a-half seniority over me gave her the edge in decision-making, so whatever she decided to do, I did. When she played with dolls, I played with dolls. When she sewed dolls' clothes, I sewed dolls' clothes. When she learned to embroider, I learned to embroider. When she decided to dress up in Mama's old clothes, I dressed up in Mama's clothes.

I remember when I got my doll. The store had many sizes and shapes, and I chose the colored one. It was rather small and had three tufts of black hair sticking out, one on top and one on each side. I named her Kinky Lee-Andre. I'll never know how I came up with a name like Lee-Andre in the cornfields of Missouri.

When I was around five years old, my mother told me that from then on it was my job to dry dishes. I was upset. I protested and cried but, in the end, I dried dishes. In those days you could yowl and protest all you wanted as long as you did what you were told. If you rebelled you were sent out to fetch a switch, which Mama would use to whip your behind. She could make a switch sing. If you brought in one too light and flimsy, she would go back out and get one that always seemed to me more like a branch. And these weren't just symbolic beatings, either. When she was through, you had welts on your behind. In those days I cried and protested a lot.

Then came the ultimate humiliation. It was now my job

to empty the chamber pot. For those of you who know only urban or modern environments, the chamber pot was a kind of enamel bucket with a lid that everyone used to piss and shit in at night or during real bad weather, instead of making the trip out back to the outhouse. It's surprising how many times it was full to the brim, and at that age I didn't have the physical strength to carry it in a way that would avoid the inevitable spills. I was condemned for life. Being the youngest, there was no one coming up behind me to pass the buck to as I grew older. Until I went to California, when I was seventeen, we never had an indoor bathroom.

Mama was a saint. She taught me that there were no bad people in the world, only those who made mistakes or stumbled along the path of righteousness. That naïve simplicity touched me to the marrow. Even today's state of the world hasn't dampened my hope in the future of our species. Mama and Papa believed that all one had to do was work hard and go to church and everything would be all right. And, of course, it didn't hurt to have a good dose of the patriotism that any other peasant from Missouri had during that time of world war. What mattered was to carry yourself in a manner that would earn the respect and approval of everyone.

That's probably why I never liked watermelon. At that time, stereotyped images of colored people always showed them with a big slice of watermelon, and I didn't want anyone to see me like that. I remember one winter, after we had moved to Sedalia to be close to a school, I went down to J. C. Penney with Mama to buy a pair of mittens. Naturally, I grabbed the red pair, my favorite color, but Mama insisted on a gray pair. I protested. Without a word or so much as a glance at me, she gave me one of the most vicious backhands in the mouth I'd ever got. It was many years later before I understood why she did that. At the time, I didn't know that red was supposed to be all niggers' favorite color.

The only music allowed at home was religious or classical. Jazz and blues was the music of the devil. Papa was an excellent tenor. Too bad he was confined to backwoods obscurity. He sang in the church choir and in a quartet of friends, and later became the director of the church choir. He would work all year long preparing for the annual Christmas and Easter cantatas. He would send off for the sheet music and then make copies by hand to distribute to members of the choir. We had an upright piano at home, and all my sisters at one time or another took piano lessons. It never appealed to me, so I was never pushed to do the same.

Papa was stern. My relationship with him consisted of hello; goodbye; yes, sir; and no, sir. Period. He was sort of a mysterious ogre that was often invoked by Mama and my sisters if I didn't behave. In other words, whatever I was doing wrong, they said they were going to tell Papa about it when he came home. That made me take on a defensive attitude toward him, and whenever he was at home I would keep as much distance between him and me as possible. Because I was always trying to do what I wanted, rather than what Mama or my sisters wanted, I was never really certain when they were going to carry out the threat to inform on me, so as far as I was concerned, Papa was someone to avoid.

The only time my fears were realized, he was home sick with something and Marleeta and I were messing around, like kids do. On all the windows and doors of the house there were fine mesh screens to keep out the flies, and Marleeta and I liked to press our lips against them as hard as we could so that when we withdrew, our lips would bear the pattern imprint of the screen. That day, Marleeta was pressing her lips into a full spread and I was standing on the other side. Looking at her like that, I just couldn't resist picking up a wooden yardstick and holding one end while pulling back on the other, aimed at her lips. She never thought I would be so callous as to let it go, but, naturally, I did.

The instant the yardstick hit her mouth I knew I had made the mistake of my life. She let out the most blood-curdling scream. Papa bounded out of bed. I froze. I knew what lay in store for me. Papa seized the yardstick and I started screaming, fearing he was going to skin me alive. He had finished whipping me and was back in bed before I realized that he hadn't hurt me at all. It was the only whipping he ever gave me. But my fear of him had kept me screaming anyway.

All social and cultural activity back then was centered on church. Sunday school and church services took up half a day on Sunday, and then there were Wednesday night prayer meetings, Friday night choir practices, and one night for the usher board. The colored church in Appleton City was one of the sources of pride for our family because it was Grandpa Joseph Cox, Papa's father, who had started it. Papa had two black metal boxes that seemed to contain all the family treasures, and among them was Grandpa Cox's preacher's license and the correspondence from the district superintendent of the Methodist church asking Grandpa to send fifty cents for a license so he could start a church.

Grandpa Cox was a special case. He was born in 1845. Someone on the plantation where he was born kept a record of when the slave women gave birth, and the page recording Grandpa's birth was also in one of the black boxes. The wife of the plantation owner taught Grandpa how to read and write—a move that was progressive at the time, and an offense punishable by law. Upon his "liberation," the simple fact of his literacy gave him a relative power and self-respect that labeled him an "uppity nigger." It was always a source of great pride in the family that a hole in the wall of a store in Osceola, Missouri—put there by a shotgun blast—bore testimony to Grandpa's objection to that appellation. He was a righteous uppity nigger, all right. As ultimate proof, he married a white woman. To do so, they had to go to the state of Kansas because interracial marriage in Missouri was illegal. Maria Müller had been brought to the States by her mother from the German-speaking part of Switzerland after her father, Jacob Müller, had died.

Unless they were ignorant of racial problems, I don't see how an eighteen-year-old Swiss immigrant would end up marrying a thirty-seven-year-old ex-slave, but somehow it happened. And the fact that Grandma Cox was white and Grandpa wasn't—the reverse of how it usually was when you had yellow niggers in the family—was held up as a source of pride in our family. These differences were strongly emphasized in the family education. I didn't grow up with any complexes about being less than anybody.

Also tucked away in the black treasure boxes was a certificate authorizing Grandpa to teach school. Here and there on the printed certificate from the Board of Education, the word "colored" had been inserted by hand to clearly define the boundaries of Grandpa's maneuverability.

For me, the fact that coloreds and whites had their own schools and churches seemed the most natural thing in the world. I used to hear the grownups talking about slavery times and lynchings, but somehow I felt insulated from all that by either time or space.

In the immediate surroundings of Appleton City there were a couple of hundred people, and everyone knew everybody else. When everyone would go into town on Saturday nights to do shopping, I didn't see any difference in the relationships between coloreds and whites. There were white friends who visited us and whom we visited. I never felt inferior to anybody. I didn't even know we were poor. One of the local families, the Braunbergers, owned the town's drugstore and had a son a couple of years older than me. His clothes were always passed on to me and were a source of happiness and anticipation; for me, such generosity did not mean that we were poor but rather that the Braunbergers were exceptionally nice people. The only time I felt lacking was the year Santa Claus forgot to drop by our house on Christmas Eve. But really, that was his fault and had nothing directly to do with us.

Mama worked hard all summer long growing everything she could, and she would spend fall canning what she had grown. Then there were the chickens and ducks, as well as the hogs that Papa butchered every now and then. I never felt we were poor, since there was always something to eat in the pantry and the smokehouse.

Finally, the great day came when I could start school. I had already spent some time there, as Mama would send us with Mary Jane whenever she had to go somewhere. It was one of those country schools that combined all the grades in the one and only classroom. The teacher would teach each grade in turn and everyone else in the room would hear what was being taught, no matter their level. This preschool experience, plus my constant presence in the same room at home where my sisters did their homework, allowed me to learn how to read and write before I officially started school. And when I did, I skipped first grade and went right into second. I started out being a proud nigger.

Because many of our neighbors had gone north, there were only three of us in class during my first year of school: my sister Marleeta; Shirley Burton, the daughter of our neighbors; and myself. We were literally being tutored privately, a state of affairs that did not last. I don't know if the funds were cut or what, but in the summer of 1943 Papa sold the farm and we moved about seventy miles northeast to Sedalia, where he started working at the Ford garage.

Sedalia was the town where Scott Joplin lived when he wrote "Maple Leaf Rag," although we hadn't heard of him yet. The only ragtime musician I had heard of was Blind Boone, and only for the simple reason that a distant relative of ours was his wife or girlfriend.

Sedalia at that time was a town with a population of about ten thousand. I don't know what percentage was colored, but at school there were around three hundred students, all classes combined, first grade through twelfth. The colored part of town was on the north side of the Missouri Pacific railroad tracks, and the line ran through town in a north-south direction, on its way between Chicago and Denver.

The railroad line had run by our house in Appleton City, too—right along the edge of the big field where Papa grew cereals to feed the animals. All the hobos moving around in those days must have marked our place because there was not one who didn't come to the house and ask for a meal. Mama never turned anyone away. She would feed them enough to last a couple of days. I remember her ritual of making up a package of ground coffee to give them when they left.

There was also a lot of military traffic on the railroad line in those days. Fort Leonard Wood was in the southern part of the state, and occasionally a train of prisoners would go by with guards on top and hanging off the sides with machine guns. I would run out with my wooden Tommy gun and pretend to mow down everyone on the train while waving my tiny American flag.

All along the edge of the field there were blackberry bushes separating our land from the railroad line. Mama made jelly, jam, and mouthwatering blackberry pies. At one time or another Junior worked as a dishwasher in a restaurant at the junction about twenty miles away. The trains stopped there to take on fuel and water while those who wanted refreshment could eat during the stopover. He would grab a freight to come home every night; they always slowed down just a little before our house before passing through Appleton City. One night he came in torn to shreds, bleeding all over, as if a lion or tiger had gotten hold of him. Having made the mistake of grabbing an express that didn't slow down, he had jumped off anyway and landed, full force, in the blackberry patch.

Junior was the hunter in the family. In Sedalia he hooked up with a couple of friends and sometimes they would go hunting several times a week. All that their respective families could not consume was sold to make a little pocket change. I was eight years old when Junior finally let me start going along to carry the game bag. The main catch was cottontail rabbits, squirrels, and quail. Heading home after the hunt, they would stop along the way and do some target shooting with Junior's .22. One day when they had all missed the target on the first shot, I asked for and was afforded a chance to try it out myself, and to everyone's surprise, including my own, I hit it! So began my love affair with guns. From then on Junior let me carry the .22 while he carried the .410. I became a fairly good shot and began to knock off my share of cottontails, breaking from their cover, moving relatively fast.

When I was ten years old, I joined the National Rifle Association. I devoured any literature dealing with firearms I could get my hands on. Even as an adult the passion stayed with me, and after I moved to California I possessed a real arsenal. It included a beautiful Winchester Model 70, caliber 30.06, with a four-power telescopic sight. Up to two hundred yards, I could pick the hairs off a gnat's ass. I used to go target practicing at a range just south of San Francisco. Most of the people on the shooting stands were members of the San Francisco Police Department, and I was always impressed with their ability. When they finished shooting at the end of the day on the pistol range of fifty yards, the centers of their targets were nothing but big holes. I shot a tight group myself and my results were as good as theirs.

The years rolled by uneventfully in peaceful Sedalia. I had good grades in school but didn't learn much, especially about anything that was going to help open doors usually closed to colored people. The dream of all young colored kids was to finish high school and move to some big city and find a job. For us, the closest was Kansas City, followed by St. Louis and, if you were really lucky, perhaps Denver or Chicago. The alternative was to enlist in a branch of the military, a sure ticket out of flat, boring Sedalia.

The summer I graduated from high school my father's brother and his wife and daughter—Uncle Harry, Aunt Rose, and my cousin Dolores—came to Sedalia on vacation from California, where they had moved about twenty years before. Dolores and I hit it off real good, and when Uncle Harry and Aunt Rose went back to California, Dolores stayed to spend the rest of the summer with us. When it was time for her to return home, Uncle Harry sent me a ticket as well as an invitation to live with them in California. Manna from heaven! California? That was like talking about going to the moon. That was someplace you never dreamed of reaching. That's the land of milk and honey, where the streets were paved with gold.

2

Long Way from Missouri

I STEPPED OFF THE TRAIN in Oakland, California, at five in the afternoon on August 27, 1953. I was wearing my best mail-order clothes, straight from Chicago: a gray tam with a blue tassel on top, a gray shirt with a blue collar and sleeves, and gray pants. I also had on my gray suede and blue-alligator wingtip shoes with two rows of white stitches. I was ready to conquer the West.

Aunt Rose was there to meet me and take me to the house in San Mateo. Just seeing the Oakland–San Francisco Bay Bridge was frightening enough, but with all that water underneath, my asshole was sucking wind. When we got to the San Francisco side of Treasure Island, the usual afternoon fog was rolling in—the kind that's thick, hugging the ground, moving fast, and enveloping everything in its path. I noticed no one else was getting excited, but my instincts were telling me to run the other way. Back home, when you saw thick clouds close to the ground like that, you knew to take cover because it meant a violent storm was coming—a tornado or something. I got up enough nerve to ask what it was, and when they told me it was just fog, it didn't help much because I'd never actually seen fog before. I wanted to know what it did. They only laughed, but that was enough to convey their lack of concern, so I calmed down.

When we arrived at the house in San Mateo, my cousin

Billy opened the door and frowned at the sight of me—hardly a warm welcome, to say the least. He was seventeen, the same age as me, and I learned right away that he would refuse to be seen with me in my current outfit. To go out with him I would have to wear some of his clothes, which, to me, were the latest thing in square: cashmere V-neck sweaters, khaki denims, and brown-and-white Oxford shoes. When he took me to the barbershop he really put one over on me. The barber was a friend of his, and without my knowledge, and without my consent, he had him cut off practically all my hair. He chopped off my rooster comb; I could have cried. Back home we kept our hair pretty short, but without ever cutting the hair right up front. We would load it up with grease and smooth it down over the top of our head, giving us the illusion of having long, wavy hair.

The next thing was to teach me how to walk. Billy didn't seem to appreciate or be impressed with my Kansas City crawl, which to me was the latest thing in cool. He and a friend, Macao Porter, would walk on each side of me, and whenever I would forget and start rocking they would pull on each shoulder to make me walk straight. After a time, the two of them got my physical appearance to where it was acceptable to them. I went along with it all because I always wanted to be hip and fit in.

San Mateo was a middle-class suburb of San Francisco, not far from San Francisco International Airport. The first thing I wanted to do was to get a job washing dishes or something at the airport, but Uncle Harry said if I wanted to stay with them I would have to enroll in the local college. If I wanted to work I would have to move out and get a place of my own. So naturally I enrolled in San Mateo Junior College.

For the first time, I was going to school with whites. Out of three thousand students there were only three blacks the first year—it was very uncomfortable, to say the least. Each new class was invited to tea by the college president, and as always, I was the perfect example of timidity. We were so many that everyone stood, and when servers came around and handed us each a cup of tea on a saucer and another small plate with a piece of cake, I didn't know what to do. As I glanced around, it seemed as if everyone else was eating and drinking, but in my nervousness and embarrassment I couldn't figure out how they were doing it with both hands full. So I just stood there and suffered. Finally, I managed to put everything down and slip away.

One Saturday night shortly after I arrived, Billy got permission to use the car. We got sharp—by his standards—and headed for San Francisco. My first impression can be summed up by one word: wow! In 1953, the North Beach section of San Francisco was like a magnet or a drug for me. I was fresh from the country and didn't understand much of what I was seeing, but the ambiance was such that I loved it at first sight. The sculptor Alexander Calder was the rage, and there was not a bar or club that didn't have a mobile or stabile in his style hanging from the ceiling. The hungry i and the Purple Onion were relaxed, cool spots in those days, and inexpensive. Soon, one of my favorite places was Miss Smith's Tea Room, up on Grant Street. I think it was a gay bar. At that time I didn't know what that meant, but I liked the warm, friendly atmosphere. Then there were the jazz clubs, the Downbeat on lower Market Street and the infamous Black Hawk. I became a regular.

To finish our evenings, we always made the pilgrimage to Fillmore Street to down some hot links or ribs and sweet potato pie at Leonard's or the Kansas City Hickory Pit, and then on to Jimbo's Bop City. After the clubs closed to the public at two in the morning, the musicians in town would stay up and jam way into the next morning. I loved it all.

The area in North Beach originally called the Barbary Coast was going by the name “the International Settlement” when I got there, and it had become a street of striptease clubs and bars. That’s where I first met jazz musician John Handy. He was playing tenor sax in one of the clubs. We always stopped by to holler at him.

To earn pocket money I started cleaning houses after classes and on weekends. After a few months I chanced upon a job washing dishes in a restaurant at night. It was there that I met “Doc.” He had recently come out of prison, where he’d served time for a drug charge; in those days the repression was fierce when it came to drug arrests. I quickly joined the fraternity and discovered the benefits of reefer, ganja, the killer weed. Together, we discovered peyote after reading Aldous Huxley’s book *The Doors of Perception*, recounting his experience with peyote.

In those days peyote wasn’t illegal; ten dollars sent to an address found in a magazine would get you a bagful. We sent off for some to conduct our own experiments. When it arrived, the bag was huge—enough to last for months. Take it from me, there is nothing on earth that tastes worse than peyote, and we would always have to struggle to get it to stay down. After about an hour, when we started feeling the effects, we would listen to records—Charlie Parker and other way-out contemporary stuff. Doc had one record of someone playing a prepared piano that made weird sounds. Doc and his friends used to talk about Sartre, philosophy, and stuff like that. I’d be sitting there, stoned out of my head, not understanding anything I heard, but it was hip to me, so I dug it and hung in.

During summer vacations I got a job at Lake Tahoe washing pots in a restaurant. Doc couldn’t get hired because he had done time, so we split the peyote and I left him behind in

San Francisco. I wouldn't see Doc again for another five years. Meanwhile, unbeknownst to us, peyote had been outlawed; maybe if we'd known, we would have made different choices. Doc wrote a friend in prison asking him if he'd like some cotton candy—code for peyote, which looks like eucalyptus seeds with a tuft of white cotton—and when the authorities who screen the letters sent to prisoners saw that, the pigs staked out Doc's pad and, while he was at work, broke in and tore the place up to find out what exactly "cotton candy" was. They found the peyote. At this same time, I had constructed a mobile of peyote buttons and had it hanging in the middle of my room in Tahoe, in the place I shared with a Liberian student, Edwin Harmon, who was a fellow dishwasher. (He was studying criminology, and upon returning to his country he eventually became head of the police.) One day when I came in from spending some time at the beach, he showed me a headline in the *San Francisco Examiner.* Doc was making history. He was the first person busted for peyote after it was outlawed. He had already done time, so they hung a heavy sentence on him; he served five years before he got paroled. I was alarmed, in part because I was uncertain whether they knew that I had the other half of the stash. My mobile and the rest of the peyote went swimming, quick, in Lake Tahoe.

San Mateo Junior College only covered the first two years of university, and after I finished my second year I decided to move to Oakland. In my free time, I hung out at the California Hotel on San Pablo Avenue near Thirty-fourth Street, where they had mambo sessions every Sunday and I ran into people like dancers Ruth Beckford, Zack Thompson, and Kaye Dunn.

I'd gone to Oakland in part because it was where my sisters Irene and Mary Jane had settled. Mary Jane was a medical secretary, and Irene's husband, Billy, was a mailman, notwithstanding his degree in business administration and experience as the director of a hospital in Kansas City. I found a room in Irene's building for twenty-five dollars a month, and since my unemployment benefits were twenty-five dollars a week, it wasn't too bad. That carried me through until I too got a job carrying mail, in December of 1955. In those days, civil service was one of the few places coloreds had a chance to get a job.

It was a funny coincidence that I became a mailman considering that the first time I was ever called "nigger" was in San Mateo by a Japanese mailman. I had leaned on his car and he shouted, "Take your hands off my car, nigger!" Remembering Mama's philosophy, I dismissed him as someone stumbling on the path of righteousness. I didn't know then that it had been only eight years since people of Japanese descent had been released from the camps they had been held in during the Second World War, after the U.S. government had made the racist decision to imprison them in the name of national security. What with that racial slur and the challenges I had faced being surrounded by whites at college (most of my white friends were gay, liked jazz, or smoked dope), I was beginning to become conscious of the dichotomy in American society. I remember the day in 1954 when the United States Supreme Court finally declared school segregation unconstitutional. We were sitting at the dinner table when we heard the news, and then Uncle Harry made a speech about how we were witnessing history being made. The real impact of that decision did not begin to sink in for me until much later, however, when Little Rock began to make headlines in the struggle for integrated schools.

Before Little Rock, though, was Montgomery, Alabama. It was there in 1955 that Rosa Parks, tired after a day's work, refused to get out of the seat she had taken in the white section of the bus. This was the spark that started the prairie fire of the civil rights movement. A young colored minister, Martin Luther King, Jr., was elected head of the boycott committee, and the Montgomery bus boycott eventually led to the Supreme Court decision, in November of 1956, that bus segregation was unconstitutional. After the court's ruling, many black churches were bombed in Alabama, but that didn't stop the momentum. After the success of the Montgomery boycott, a new civil rights organization was formed, called the Southern Christian Leadership Conference (SCLC). Martin Luther King, Jr., was elected as its head.

I was hearing about all those things beginning to happen in the South, but, as before, I was insulated from getting involved, both by geography and by my own ignorance. For me, these were more or less just interesting events in the news. The one story that had really jolted me was when Emmett Till, of Chicago, was visiting relatives in the South and was lynched for supposedly whistling at a white woman. He was fourteen years of age. That was the first time I felt that maybe Mama's philosophy might be wrong. That was in the summer of 1955.

In the fall of 1957, Governor Orval Faubus of Arkansas called out the state national guard to prevent Negro students from entering Central High School in Little Rock. The conflict became so tense that President Eisenhower was obliged to send in federal troops to force the desegregation of Central and to protect the nine Negro students who were involved. The guard remained there for the school year of 1957–58, and Faubus finally closed all schools the next year rather than desegregate them. But the process had begun and would soon spread to most of the South. Another significant event occurred in 1957, in Africa. Ghana, the former "Gold Coast," became independent.

Now that I was making what I considered real money, I got clean. My cousin Billy's taste had really worn off on me, and now I looked Ivy League all the way. If it wasn't British, I didn't want it. I wore all my hair cut off and was going around with a clean head. According to Iris Vaughn, whom I later married, that was the reason she was attracted to me at a party and had wanted to meet me. We couldn't seem to cool off our hot pants, so we got hitched after a short courtship.

Iris was from a rather economically secure family and was the only child at home. She had a brother, a dentist in Texas, and her mother had big plans to send her only daughter off to some bourgeois Negro university to find a "good" husband, but then here came a mailman. The night we told her we were married, my new mother-in-law chased me out of the house with the biggest butcher knife I had ever seen. She started throwing Iris's clothes out the door, into the rain that was coming down like cats and dogs. We scooped up everything and split to my pad on Fifty-third Street in Oakland—one room with a Murphy bed.

Iris was a student at San Francisco City College, and every day after classes she would go by her mother's house to see if things had improved. Every time, her mother would open the door, hit her in the mouth, then slam the door shut. After a few weeks of that I felt the need to do my husbandly duty and defend my wife, so I went with her. Not wanting to stretch things, I parked the car a few houses away. This time, when her mother opened the door, she pushed past Iris, jumped into her car, and burned rubber until she had pulled up just beside me. I thought I would shit. I didn't know if she was going to pull out a gun. To my surprise, she smiled and said, "Why don't you come on in?" It was clear she had made her peace with our marriage.

Financially, we weren't making it at all with the $110 I was getting every fifteen days. Iris's mother offered us a room in her home in San Francisco, and we accepted. Those were strained times. By now Iris was getting fat with pregnancy.

In the meantime I was getting quite expert at detecting which letters had cash in them. Some letters had that special spongy feeling when there are several loose bills together in an envelope. I quickly began to supplement my miserable income.

After about a year my employers were on my case. And I knew it. They started planting letters with cash in them, but I was so cocky by then that I was ripping off even the plants. Usually, I would go to a toilet somewhere, open the letters, put the money in my pocket, and flush everything else down. When the fatal day arrived, I had ripped off two letters but only opened one and put the other in my pocket to open later. That was the day they decided to see if they could catch me dirty.

That wasn't the first time I had been busted. Back in Sedalia, during my four years of high school, I had worked at the grocery store on our side of the tracks. During the school year I was paid six dollars a week for four hours of work a day, plus twelve hours on Saturday. In the summer, I was paid ten dollars a week for twelve hours a day, six days a week. For that I did deliveries and also worked as a stock boy, janitor, and cashier. I never got a raise, so I regularly supplemented my income from the cash register. My boss, Mr. Kantor, knew it. He accepted it because I never exaggerated and I was a good worker, and everything went fine for four years, until it was time for my graduation ceremonies from high school. There were expenses that I just couldn't cover with my salary, and I didn't even consider asking Papa, since I had started working at the age of thirteen and had always had to pay for anything I wanted or needed. So, when I closed the store the night before the graduation ceremonies, I left the back door open and returned after midnight. That time I took the whole moneybag. I knocked stuff around to make it look like a burglary, then stashed the bag in the weeds in the alley behind the house and went to bed.

The next morning I decided to take my shoes downtown for a professional shine. I wanted to be as sharp as possible for my graduation. In going up the alley, I couldn't resist picking up the moneybag and putting it in my pocket. On my way back home I saw a police car coming and didn't really pay it any attention until it approached and I saw Mama in the backseat. They pulled alongside of me and Mama said that Mr. Kantor wanted to see me. The two policemen were silent. As soon as we entered the store the policemen started searching me and pulled out the bag. They immediately put my hands behind my back and put on the handcuffs. Mama started screaming, "My baby, my baby!" I started crying and the police drove off with me, siren wailing. What a drama! While everyone was at high school for the ceremonies, I was in the city jail, in a cell straight from the Middle Ages: dirty, worn stone walls and a floor that looked like it hadn't ever been cleaned. Hanging from the wall on chains there was a cot made from metal strips woven together, and a hole in the middle of the floor for a toilet. Whoever had been in the cell before must have been crazy or something because there was dried shit all over the walls, ceiling, and floor, with feathers stuck in it. I don't know what that was about.

That evening my uncle—the only black doctor in town and highly respected—came to get me out of jail. The policeman released me to him and he drove me home. When we pulled up in front of the house it looked like someone had died. All the relatives and neighbors were there. They were fanning Mama, and I guess they thought they were giving me words of encouragement, but all I wanted to do was hide. I didn't leave the house until the family insisted that I return to school. Even though classes were over, school was not officially out until Friday, but I was really ashamed to face my friends. On Wednesday I finally went back, and when I arrived I was, to my amazement and confusion, welcomed as a hero. That was my first brush with the law. But the second time, in Oakland, things were different.

I spent twenty-four hours in jail before Iris managed to raise the hundred dollars of bail money. She couldn't ask her parents; we weren't about to tell them what had happened. After that, I immediately got a job driving city buses in San Francisco. When I finally went before a judge, I think it helped that I had a job and Iris was pregnant. I got five years probation.

During that time, I made friends with another bus driver, who lived half a block down the street. He drove San Francisco cable cars and had dreams about making films. One day he asked me to go with him to the Marina's Yacht Harbor to help him try to simulate some underwater scenes. We were only in knee-deep water, but he was trying to film in such a way as to give the illusion of being in deeper water. He had an old Bolex camera wrapped in plastic bags held closed with rubber bands to try to keep it watertight. His name: Melvin Van Peebles, the man who went on to write, direct, and act in dozens of movies and plays, including the groundbreaking *Sweet Sweetback's Baadasssss Song* from 1971.

My career as a bus driver came to an end a year later when the department of personnel ran a check on me and found out I had lied on my application. I said I hadn't been busted before, but of course that wasn't true. Inspectors came and pulled me off the bus I was driving.

By that time, my daughter, Kimberly, was born, and I couldn't find a job, and neither could Iris. We had no marketable skills. I was getting forty dollars a week in unemployment compensation when I decided to go back to the university to acquire some skill that would allow me to be independent and not have to worry about the fact that I had been busted. With so many doors closed to Negroes, to be a professional was to become a doctor, dentist, or lawyer. I didn't like the idea of working in a court, for obvious reasons, so I decided to register as a predental student at the University of California at Berkeley. I had been taught by my parents that if you were determined to do something, nothing could stop you from doing it. I truly believed that.

At the beginning of my second semester at Cal, I was forced to take a job or lose my unemployment check, and I was convinced I could deal with both a job and my classes. A friend, Willie Little, got me a job as an offset press operator in the place he worked. The job paid forty dollars a week, which was exactly what I was getting from unemployment. That hurt, but I had no other choice. It was hard to both work and go to class, and after a couple of months, I was about dead from exhaustion. That was when I lost my first illusions and it became obvious to me that determination is no guarantee of success. I applied for and received an honorable dismissal from Cal with every intention of returning at the first opportunity—which never materialized.

Working a lot of overtime, Iris and I were able to finally stand on our own feet. The first priority was to get our own pad—a two-room apartment across the street from Iris's mother. Then Iris got a job as a keypunch operator at Union Oil. Finally, we could breathe for a minute. We even bought a car—a Triumph TR3. We hardly ever put the top up. As Edith Austin once said, "You might be cold, but you're cool."

About that time I met Mark Hanson, a tall, thin, slightly round-shouldered, mustachioed white man who wore thin metal-rim glasses. He had moved to San Francisco from Los Angeles because of the McCarthy anticommunist witch hunts, since every time he found a job or a pad, the FBI would pay a visit to his boss or landlord and he would find himself out on the streets. So he moved to San Francisco. He started to work with us as an Addressograph operator, working the machine that stamped addresses on envelopes. We hit it off immediately, even though I didn't understand a lot of the political stuff he was talking about all the time.

Mark was surprised and disturbed when he discovered I was ignorant of so much of what was going on around me. He started bringing me books to read about the history of Negroes in America. Most were by the historians W. E. B. Du Bois and Herbert Aptheker. When he brought me Du Bois's *Black Reconstruction in America*, I was a little discouraged because I had never picked up a book that big before. It took me six months to get through it. I am forever grateful to Mark for opening this world to me.

In December of 1959, Fidel Castro's revolutionaries seized power in Cuba (their work for the enfranchisement of blacks was widely admired by this country's civil rights movement), and then in February of 1960, four Negro college students sat in at a Woolworth's lunch counter in Greensboro, North Carolina, demanding to be served. And with that, the civil rights movement in the United States was under way in earnest. The Congress of Racial Equality (CORE) began to organize "Freedom Rides" into the South with the purpose of desegregating interstate transport and terminals. At the end of 1961, the Interstate Commerce Commission (ICC) finally decreed that all racial segregation on interstate trains and buses must end. That also applied to waiting rooms, and carriers were forbidden to use segregated terminals.

Walking on Market Street close to my work one day, I ran into my old friend Doc, who had just gotten out of the joint. It was a warm reunion, and as we talked, we found we had something new in common. Doc had been bitten by the photography bug, and through my job at the printing shop, I had too. We began stalking the streets of San Francisco together on weekends, looking for subjects, and I rented a flat and turned it into a lab and studio. The great Henri Cartier-Bresson was my idol, and his book *The Decisive Moment* held me spellbound. I was disturbed, however, by his disdain for doing his own lab work. I got so much pleasure from seeing my images develop that I couldn't conceive of a photographer not doing his own lab work. In those days, I was a fan of Ansel Adams's technical series, *The Camera*, *The Negative*, and *The Print,* and Adams too believed that doing one's own lab work was sacred.

When a rare-photo exhibit came to the Museum of Modern Art on Van Ness Avenue, that was my first chance to see professional photographic prints. I took one look and was speechless. Up until that time I had only seen our own prints, and now before me were eight-by-ten contact prints made from eight-by-ten negatives by pioneering photographer Edward Weston. I almost decided to throw my cameras away.

Out in the world beyond my studio, the civil rights movement was really picking up steam. Negroes were sitting in all over the place. In the fall of 1962, whites rioted in Oxford, Mississippi, when James Meredith entered the University of Mississippi as its first Negro student. President Kennedy sent in five thousand army troops and federalized the state's national guard to patrol the streets of Oxford.

I was also reading more. While I was laid up a couple of

months with a case of pericarditis, I got into an author I hadn't heard of before: James Baldwin. I was given a couple of his books—*The Fire Next Time* and *Nobody Knows My Name*—by my friend Nancy, who had come from New York after marrying my friend John Handy, who had just returned from a several-years' stay on the East Coast playing with Charles Mingus. John and Nancy had met at the Blue Note jazz club, where she was working. Baldwin's writings were real eye-openers. Up until then most everything I had read was history, but Baldwin was dealing with today. I had never heard the situation of Negroes articulated in such an eloquent, forceful manner. Fortunately, I had recovered enough to attend his event when he swung through San Francisco on a speaking tour. Nancy, John, Mark, Willie—we all went to hear him.

The big March on Washington was being planned at that time, and of everyone in our group of friends, it was John who made the trip in August of 1963. He had hardly been back a week when the church bombing in Birmingham, Alabama, blew four little Negro girls out of this world. That was the straw that broke my back. That was too much. I had never felt such a sensation of impotency. Action was the only thing that could soothe my feelings, and I had to figure out what I could do. Willie, Mark, Nancy, John, and I decided to try to raise some money to send down to the SCLC in Alabama. John knew most of the musicians in town, and those he didn't, Nancy did. So it was a natural idea to do a benefit concert. With one week's work we managed to draw enough people to raise $1,300. Singer Carmen McRae, pianist Ahmad Jamal, saxophonists Sonny Rollins and Brew Moore, and John made up the program. Too bad it wasn't recorded.

The benefit relieved some immediate pressure, but what could we do for the long run? At the time, CORE appeared to be the most dynamic civil rights organization in San Francisco, so we all joined.

It was around this time that I had begun to hear of Malcolm X, the Black Muslim minister. He seemed to be a bad nigger. They were always putting him on TV or the radio with some Uncle Tom or an endorsed spokesman for the system. I really admired the way he would eat them up and spit them out in little pieces, all the while remaining cool, calm, and polite. I didn't know it then, but his ideas would become important to our later efforts in the struggle.

I didn't last long in CORE—maybe around six months—but it was long enough to be elected as chairman of the public-relations committee. It was one of those elections where someone is nominated and then nominations are immediately closed because no one wants the job. You're in by acclamation. We did manage to turn out some nice newsletters, in part because we went to my job after-hours, going in after dark and working all night to produce our pages before the employees arrived the next morning.

Some token gains were made, and the local movement grew pretty big, with sit-ins at the Palace Hotel and the Cadillac dealership to protest their discriminatory hiring practices. I had noticed that whenever a new door was opened, the person who inevitably got the job was always someone who was already making it, while the people who really needed work were never chosen. I was proud to be part of the movement hoping to change that.

The assassination of President Kennedy in November of 1963 rocked the country, with ramifications felt all the way down to the Black Muslims. Malcolm X was suspended from the Nation of Islam when he said of Kennedy's death, "Looks like the chickens are coming home to roost," meaning the president had gotten his due. Although Malcolm's suspension was received with shock at the time, it allowed him to develop his own ideas. Only then some felt he was becoming too clairvoyant. They had to kill him, and a few years later they did. A Nation of Islam gunman assassinated Malcolm X on February 21, 1965.

I left CORE. In the struggle for integration I was seeing only token results; most of the integration I saw at the time was between the sheets. I didn't know what to do, but I felt certain that CORE wasn't the vehicle that was going to do it, so I split.

I didn't see anything else around that seemed to be dealing with the problems either, so I plunged back into photography. It became a real passion. I hooked up with Doc and we started stalking the streets again. Around that time I saw a book that had published the images of several photographers—Dorothea Lange, Gordon Parks, and Ben Shahn, among others—who had been sent by the government to document the conditions brought about by the Great Depression and the drought that had devastated the Dust Bowl region. Those photographs touched me to the point that I decided to try to make images that would translate the contradictions of being black in America.

I let the flat go and got a nice big second-floor loft on Natoma Street, close to the unemployment office. I set up a real good lab and studio. It was mostly for my personal pleasure, but to justify it, I used contacts I had acquired through my job to get some advertising work. My first paying job was photographing a can of tuna for the firm McCann Erickson in San Francisco. I did a lot of set-up shots (now called packshots), and they were extremely well-paying: seventy-five dollars for an eight-by-ten black-and-white print back in 1964 and 1965 wasn't too bad.

Doc needed a pad, so I invited him to make himself a corner in the studio. He brought around a friend of his, Ed Newell, who had also done some time. Ed was into watercolors and had

had a couple of successful shows, but he too had been bitten by the photo bug, so we got along. Then there was Larry Billips, whom I had met at the store where I bought my supplies. We started stalking the streets as four.

I was still married to Iris, but I had a girlfriend on the side—Lee Anna Brown—who lived in Marin City. I used to hang out on the "bottom" over there and managed to make some interesting images. But I wasn't getting the satisfaction I had anticipated. On New Year's Day of 1966, while driving in San Francisco down Webster Street at Ellis, I saw a whole block of houses that had recently been torn down for redevelopment. That left exposed the rear of the block of houses facing the other street over. It looked like something from *Tobacco Road*. It looked like the wood had never had a coat of paint and everything had an aspect of decay. On one or two back porches, wash hanging on makeshift clotheslines added to the poverty of it all. Right in the middle of the block, parked in lonely splendor, was a shiny new Coupe de Ville Cadillac. Instinctively, I knew this was the type of image I had been looking for. I stopped my car in the middle of the street, jumped out, and fired away with my Hasselblad 500C.

Seeing the first print coming up in the developer was a religious experience. I got goosebumps all over. Finally, after all the time and effort, here was an image worthy of the goal I had set for myself. I really milked the cow with that one. I stayed in the lab for about a week making prints, from eight-by-tens to twenty-by-twenty-fours.

3

Just Another Nigger

Little did I know it, but that shot of the back porches and the Cadillac was to be my last image. When I hit the streets again, I roamed around all day not tripping the shutter one time. I'm not a psychologist, so I can't explain it in technical terms, but it was almost as if having made that one strong image, I wasn't able to see anything else that matched it in intensity. I knew every shot couldn't be a masterpiece, but I found I just couldn't trip the shutter anymore if the image was not translating that same reality, and with that same force. I couldn't understand it at the time. My overall feeling was frustration and confusion. Perhaps unconsciously I knew already that simply recording history was not enough for me.

I stopped going to the studio and no longer went out looking for images. I was out of it. Total frustration. I wasn't even going around to see Doc and the others. Doc moved and started staying in a small studio behind our friend Ed Newell's house.

I was searching for answers or some philosophy that would give me the peace of mind I so desperately wanted. I read a book about the life of an Indian yogi named Paramahansa Yogananda, and it was interesting, but I really didn't want to withdraw from the world in that way. I then picked up something Doc had previously turned me on to: a book by P. D. Ouspensky dealing with the teachings of philosopher George Gurdjieff. I found that one a little more interesting simply because, one day while lying down reading the book, something distracted me and as I was bringing my consciousness out of the book I realized that some ear, somewhere inside me, had been listening to the music coming from the radio and I was patting my foot to the rhythm without knowing it. That illustrated one of the aspects of Gurdjieff's teachings, which was the existence of different centers of consciousness. I was impressed, but still, for me, that wasn't the answer either.

That year, 1965, was also a heavy year politically. In February, Malcolm X had been shot down while making a speech at a meeting in Harlem, and I remember seeing a photograph circulated by the news media across the country showing one of his bodyguards giving him mouth-to-mouth resuscitation. Three years later, the same individual would join the Black Panther Party in New York, and still later, we would learn at the trial of the New York 21, which would consume me for several years, that he was a policeman. After he had graduated from the police academy he was never put into uniform but instead sent directly to Harlem to establish a reputation as a militant. For a number of years, he served his masters well.

Also in February of 1965, a civil rights worker named Jimmie Lee Jackson was lynched in Selma, Alabama, and a protest march was organized from Selma to the capitol in Montgomery. The night after the march ended, a white woman was killed by a shotgun blast while driving some blacks back to Selma.

This was also the year that the Voting Rights Act was finally passed by Congress. There were many vicious murders, lynchings, beatings, bombings, and arrests of black people before that bill was passed to finally give us the vote. It was Malcolm X who said, "It will either be the ballot or the bullet."

In spring of that year, the big demonstrations started against the war in Vietnam. The one in San Francisco was the biggest

I had ever seen, with marchers stretched out from the Ferry Building to Golden Gate Park for hours before the last of them finally arrived. That was the first march I ever participated in. I was timid and carried my cameras to hide behind.

For me, the most significant event of 1965 was the August uprising in the Watts section of Los Angeles. Again, as in New York in 1964, the people of the black community rebelled after an incident involving white policemen. After five days, there were "officially" around forty dead, with more than a thousand wounded and over four thousand arrested. Property damage was more than $40 million. While watching scenes of destruction and flames billowing up live on TV, I admit to having felt joy—joy and pride at seeing blacks finally saying, by their actions, that they were fed up and weren't going to sit idly by and accept an unacceptable situation. I don't think there was any event that had more influence on the course of events concerning black people for the next few years than the Watts Rebellion.

One day I got a phone call from Larry telling me they had found Doc's body in the studio behind Ed's house. He had overdosed on heroin. Doc wasn't a junkie; he only used it every now and then, and if he did find himself using it too frequently and becoming dependent, he would clean up right away. He was never really strung out on a daily basis. In the heroin trade, each time the drug changes hands between the producer and the consumer it is cut with a product to increase its volume and, therefore, the profits. One gets accustomed to certain cuts and then takes doses accordingly, usually with the desired results. But somehow, every so often, a quantity of heroin gets through to the consumer that hasn't been cut, or maybe only cut very little. Doc's last shot was pure stuff. Taking the same quantity he was used to taking cut, he didn't even have time to empty the whole syringe. When he was found he still had the needle in his vein.

In January of 1966 a worker for the Student Nonviolent Coordinating Committee (SNCC) named Sammy Younge was murdered because he wanted to use the toilet at a service station that was reserved for whites. That was in Tuskegee, Alabama. Three years later, civil rights activist and SNCC's executive secretary James Forman wrote a book about Sammy's life: *Sammy Younge, Jr.: The First Black College Student to Die in the Black Liberation Movement*, the first of several books he would write about social justice and economic equality as it relates to black Americans.

Also in June of 1966, James Meredith—the student who had integrated the University of Mississippi in 1962, set out on the March Against Fear from Memphis, Tennessee, to Jackson, Mississippi. He didn't get far before he was shot down on the road, and it was while he recovered from his wounds that a march was organized in his honor with the assistance of numerous civil rights organizations. It was during that march that SNCC worker Willie Ricks first shouted out the slogan calling for "Black Power." As the result of distortions by the news media, the slogan was wrongly attributed to Stokely Carmichael, and most people to this day think it was Stokely who first used the term. He had been elected chairman of SNCC the same summer and had turned out to be a rather articulate militant, and so it made sense that the news media did everything it could to make him look worse than he really was.

On September 27, 1966, a policeman shot a black sixteen-year-old boy to death, in the back, in the Hunters Point neighborhood of San Francisco. The people on the hill quickly applied the lesson they had learned from watching the Watts Rebellion on television and took their anger and frustration into the streets. The reaction spread to our neighborhood in the Fillmore District, and again I felt gratified seeing black people letting it all hang out. The night things spread to the Fillmore, I sat on the front steps and enjoyed the spectacle of young blacks playing cat and mouse with the police patrols. I felt, instinctively, that some process had begun that was going to change things for all times to come.

On the work side, I was a successful nigger. I never left my job at the printing shop, even with the freelance work, and my employers either never ran a check on me or didn't care that I had a record. I was a member of the San Francisco Chamber of Commerce, the California State Chamber of Commerce, and the Christian Business Men's Association, among other organizations, and I had worked my way up through the place to the title of production manager. In practice, I was the boss; there was no one on the premises over me. I had a meeting once a month to go over the books with the owner in his office, at a separate location, but the rest of the time I was on my own. I liked not having to punch a clock anymore, but I just couldn't deal with giving orders to friends with whom I had worked for years.

But it had its positive side. Now that I was doing the hiring and firing I was able to get rid of a racist who didn't want no nigger telling him what to do. The best part was being able to hire underprivileged people. I was able to hire ex-convicts through the halfway-house program and from the San Francisco office of the National Urban League, which had a program that dealt with the handicapped. That helped to ease my conscience.

It was through my experience as a boss that one day, as suddenly as you flip a switch, I finally understood that it was the system that was all wrong. I realized that it was my job to sell our services at the highest price possible, while at the same time keeping the workers' salaries as low as possible. I became aware of this while I was in the process of fighting tooth and nail with the owner for raises for everyone. His arguments were never based on the productivity or longevity of the workers. It was always a question of profit. I was elated to have made my new discovery, but the question then was how did one go about changing the system? I didn't really understand what revolution was all about. Communism and socialism were even less comprehensible to me. I was so overjoyed by my epiphany, however, that I wanted to shout it to the world.

The leaps in my political consciousness really started taking bounds at that time. I don't recall any single specific catalyst—it was probably the sum total of all my experience—but the day finally dawned when I realized that no matter how I dressed, no matter how I carried myself, when I left the small circle of people who knew me and walked down the street, I was *just another nigger*. I was thirty-one years old. Like they say, better late than never.

And then I got mad. I started organizing group discussions between blacks and whites I knew. The discussions were interesting and stimulating, but it was soon evident that this alone wasn't going to change anything. It was at one such meeting that I met Stephania. She came with her boyfriend and I was married, but I was instantly attracted by her sharp intellect and her beauty. She was looking for a job, so I hired her immediately. Although she was more than qualified to do the job, my real motivation was just to be in her presence. Discussions with Stephania were also informative. She introduced me to Frantz Fanon and his book *The Wretched of the Earth*, about the lasting effects of colonization. She also made me aware of the work of writer and critic LeRoi Jones (later Amiri Baraka).

One morning upon arriving at work Stephania looked at me, smiled, didn't say a word, and handed me the morning paper.

There, on the front page, was a photograph of niggers with guns at the state capitol in Sacramento. Niggers with guns! I couldn't believe my eyes. I devoured the article and learned that the group called itself the Black Panther Party for Self-Defense, and they were advocating that black people should be allowed to arm themselves, specifically for self-defense against racist police. I immediately thought of my arsenal at home. I started asking around to see what I could learn about these Panthers. No one I knew seemed to have heard of them, and what's more, they thought they must be crazy. Niggers with guns!

I learned that in a couple of weeks there was to be a Black Power conference in Los Angeles, and I decided to go. Stephania and her boyfriend agreed to accompany me, only Stephania couldn't attend the actual conference because it was open only to blacks. She stayed with friends while her boyfriend and I went to the conference.

I couldn't believe my eyes. The conference had gathered together the most beautiful black people I had ever seen—fancy afro hairdos, African clothes, and all. And it seemed that everyone who was someone in the movement was there: Stokely Carmichael, H. Rap Brown, LeRoi Jones, James Forman, Ron Karenga, and others. I had heard of Stokely, Rap, and LeRoi, but not the others. On the last day, the Panthers showed. I bought their newspaper, *The Black Panther*, and read it so many times I knew it by heart.

During the weekend I heard blacks talk of revolution, killing our oppressors, going back to Africa, the whole works. I was drunk with this new world I had not even known existed. Pieces started falling into place. It was a cascade, a snowball rolling down the mountainside. I was speechless. My mind was blown.

During the drive back to San Francisco, Stephania sat up front. She and her boyfriend had had an argument about something and he had lain down in the back and wouldn't talk. After a few miles I couldn't contain it any longer and I started running off at the mouth and literally crying like a baby, so full of so much new information and inspiration. Everything I had heard during the weekend helped me understand that all the efforts I had made up until then to be acceptable to mainstream society had just made me a "good nigger." I was simultaneously ashamed and furious. All I could do was cry.

Upon arriving home from work the next day, I heard loud noises coming from the ground-floor apartment that we were letting Iris's cousin use. It sounded as if a room full of people were all talking at the same time. I also smelled the inimitable odor of the killer weed. I took off my coat, loosened my tie, and went downstairs to ask for a hit. The room was full and you could cut the smoke with an axe. It was obvious that I was an intruder, since everyone immediately shut up. I asked to be passed a joint, and after a while everyone began to relax and forget about me, and pretty soon they began talking again, all at the same time. Mixed with the music coming from the record player, it was like a magma of sound. I was only interested in getting my head feeling good, so I wasn't really listening at first, but then something I heard caught my ear and I turned my attention to what was being said. It was then that I realized everyone in the room was recounting their personal histories of having been fucked over by either some policeman or judge or someone they had been or were still working for.

I ran upstairs, gathered up several of my guns and the Black Panther newspaper I had bought in Los Angeles, and took them back down to the gathering. And that was the beginning.

4

Mystery Phantom Sniper

We studied the Panther paper line by line. Many in the group were school dropouts and couldn't read effectively, so we went no faster than the slowest one could understand. Everyone seemed to enjoy the brief rundown on the functioning of firearms. Most of their experiences with guns, if any, had been with the "Saturday night special" variety. Everyone agreed that we should start meeting on a regular basis and begin searching for literature dealing with the history of black people in America and black people generally. There was an urgent necessity, felt by all, to break the chains of ignorance about our own history. I sold all my camera equipment and bought several Sears-brand bolt-action twelve-gauge shotguns. I needed to get everyone armed and accustomed to weapons as fast as possible.

We started by going out hunting jackrabbits, which was an effective way to teach the use of and respect for firearms. Those who showed particular promise became responsible for instructing others. In addition to learning the proper use and maintenance of arms, we studied black history.

It wasn't long before we had a chance to take our ideas public. San Francisco police had set up an ambush on a planned holdup at a motel, and they had called in television, radio, and newspaper reporters to capture the action. When the suspected would-be robber showed up, they shot him down in cold blood, live on television. The victim was a seventeen-year-old black youth from the Fillmore District, and several in our group knew him personally, or knew his friends. Everyone was enraged and wanted to do something. We decided it would be good to go into the streets, find his friends, and try to convince them of the need to arm themselves for self-defense, and possibly some of them would want to join us in our larger effort.

We wrote a leaflet that used this blatant murder as an example of the treatment in store for blacks if they did not arm themselves and increase their vigilance. We went to my job after-hours and printed up several thousand copies, and the next day, we hit the streets in search of the friends of the murder victim and distributed our leaflets. That was the first direct political action our group took. The brutal nature of the murder convinced us of the need to demonstrate that it was possible to arm oneself and be in the open about it. We always kept our guns in our cars as we moved around, but when we found the victim's friends in a park, we decided to carry them openly. I knew the gun laws due to my past passion of target shooting and hunting, and I knew that it was perfectly legal to walk around openly with arms in hand; back then, there was a restriction on concealing your weapons. Unfortunately, most black people were, and still are, ignorant of gun laws, and I guess we appeared to be more audacious than we really were.

Being in the open, in direct contact with people, had a positive effect. It helped us overcome a certain shyness and, more important, gave us the chance to test our ideas against reality. As we gained confidence, we decided to operate openly as an organized group and move all over town.

We had some small solid-black buttons made, and as we moved from neighborhood to neighborhood we distributed them and the leaflets. Our sessions consisted of discussions of black history and current events relevant to black people, and we always ended with a demonstration of the use of weapons.

It was at one such gathering that Sam Napier made himself known. He started rapping about Malcolm X and turned us on to the Socialist Workers Party bookstore, where all the literature on Malcolm, plus records of his speeches, was available. What a find for us. Malcolm's records became invaluable organizing tools, and his autobiography became required reading. It was thanks to Sam that we found Malcolm's works.

Nevertheless, Sam got on my shit list quick. Not long after we met, we were having one of our weekly community sessions when word came that a resident had just been arrested for not having paid a traffic ticket. Sam had the excellent idea of canvassing the neighborhood and asking for donations to bail out the brother. Everyone went to work, and in less than ten minutes we had the required amount. Sam hollered out, "Everyone to City Hall to free the brother!" By that time there was a respectable crowd and it looked like the whole community was heading out. When all the cars were loaded and it was time to pull off, Sam said goodbye, telling us he had to leave. I opened my jacket to expose my piece and asked him to get into the car, which he did, and together we went and bailed out the brother. I was always leery of those who ran their mouths and then disappeared when it was time to put their words into action.

It was around that time that in Newark, New Jersey, a white policeman arrested a black taxicab driver on some traffic charge and took him to a police station, where he was terribly beaten. Word passed by radio, from taxi to taxi, until it finally reached the community. From July 12 to July 17, 1967, the people rebelled. After it was all over there were more than twenty dead, including six women and two infants. The body of one black teenager had forty-five bullet wounds.

About the same time, we were learning more about larger uprisings, including the Cuban Revolution under Fidel Castro in the 1950s, which we read about in Che Guevara's book *Guerilla Warfare*, and also the Chinese Revolution, which we studied using the *Little Red Book* by Mao Tse-tung. With those documents, plus Malcolm's autobiography and Black Panther cofounder Huey P. Newton's essay "The Correct Handling of a Revolution," we began preparing ourselves for the war of liberation that we considered imminent. We were hearing news reports of Stokely making revolutionary statements during his travels to Havana and Hanoi, and H. Rap Brown, who had been elected the chairman of SNCC, was really rapping now, saying, "Burn, baby, burn." With small, individual rebellions jumping off across the country, we redoubled our preparations. We were convinced that we were running behind and needed to catch up. We were eager to make contact with the Panthers in Oakland, but we didn't yet feel worthy to be in their presence. There was still much work to be done. So far, we had only talked and informed and armed ourselves, but we hadn't yet proved ourselves on the firing line.

We didn't consider ourselves an organization in the traditional sense. We had no structure, no leaders, no officers. When there was a task to perform, the person most knowledgeable about the particular thing was responsible for it. So far, doing it that way had never presented any problems.

Naturally, I knew our entire group wouldn't have to participate in military activity, but how would I find out who would go along with such actions? Keeping things on a need-to-know basis to ensure security, I decided to see which members of the group might be interested in getting down to more serious business. I was convinced it was necessary to move as fast as possible to form this smaller group and begin working together in order to weld the necessary unity and confidence that would permit our eventual engagement in military activities. I had already noticed that whenever we were just sitting around talking we would manage to assemble a fairly large group, but whenever some kind of action was called for, like when we started going out to distribute leaflets, those numbers were greatly reduced. I needed to find people who were serious and committed to the cause.

Among those who were consistently present, I began to talk about the need to do something besides just talk. I observed their reactions, and of those who seemed to be the most determined, I chose to directly broach the subject of military action with only two. Their reaction was immediate and positive. The three of us then made a point of getting together, seemingly casually, after the larger gatherings had concluded, so we could talk things over.

Soon we began to do small-risk actions, mainly arsons and burglaries. The spoils from the burglaries were always sold to the community at very low prices, and the receipts were used to buy arms and ammunition. We didn't want anyone to be unarmed because of a lack of funds. Later, our group also began to sell weed to raise funds for arms and ammunition. At that time, lids (one-ounce bags) were selling for twenty dollars, so to build up steady customers and to become known, we put our lids on the market for ten dollars. We also tried our hand at making small bombs with varying degrees of success. Fortunately, we never had an accident.

It was around that time, in the summer of 1967, that the biggest rebellion to date broke out, in Detroit. From news reports it seemed like the people of Detroit were very combative. They kicked the police's behinds, the state troopers' behinds, and the national guard's behinds. For three days the rebellion went uncontained, until the 101st Airborne was brought in, units of which were also fighting in Vietnam at the time. The toll in Detroit was also the heaviest of any similar action so far, with more than forty killed, thousands wounded and arrested, and millions of dollars in damage. The war was really on.

Someone in our group knew Emory Douglas, a San Francisco artist who was known to be a member of the Black Panther Party. We asked Emory to ask Huey Newton, the twenty-five-year-old cofounder of the Panthers, if he would come speak at one of our group's meetings. He accepted with enthusiasm and the meeting was a great success. Finally, we had met and heard Huey in person. But we still didn't feel confident enough to establish a closer relationship with the Panthers. We felt we had first to prove ourselves worthy.

The three of us started hanging out together on a regular basis. We began discussing what we could do as a significant action. It was well into August when we remembered that soon it would be the anniversary of the murder of the young black man on Hunters Point that had sparked the San Francisco rebellion the year before. We decided to launch our first operation on that anniversary. There was no propaganda machinery in place to exploit our action, so the action would have to speak for itself, loudly and clearly.

One idea that we felt the community could support would be to locate the policeman who had committed the murder and execute him on the anniversary of the killing. We began researching newspapers from the year before, in the public library, to find out who and where the murderer was. We worked hard, but all we could come up with was the fact that he had been transferred to the Ingleside police station. We were unable to get a photograph of him, so we didn't know what he looked like. What to do?

Since we couldn't identify the individual policeman responsible, and since time was short, as there were only a couple weeks left before the anniversary, we concluded that there was no alternative but to launch an attack upon the station itself. The conditions of the terrain around the Ingleside station were exceptionally favorable—it was located in a park right next to the freeway—and that would facilitate our escape, which we considered the determining factor in the success or failure of any action of a military nature. The negative factor was that if we were not lucky enough to get the actual assassin, the action might not be a clear message for the people. If the police did their homework properly, however, at least they would know why it had happened. And if that helped save one black life, then the action would be worth it. We went to work.

In reconnoitering the area around the station we discovered a parking lot at San Francisco City College, located on the hill on the other side of the freeway, just overlooking the police station. That offered a nice, clear shot, but to ensure a safe getaway, we would have only one chance. It looked like the distance was around 150 yards, which meant we needed our best marksman. So, following the principle that each action should be led by the person most knowledgeable about the particular subject, I would be the one to squeeze the trigger. The work of the others was equally important, however: one person was to stay behind the wheel with the motor running, and the other was to be in the backseat holding the door open for me. After I fired I would dive into the car and the comrade in the back would help pull me in and close the door while the driver burned rubber to get away. Just preceding the action we were to steal a car to use, and of course we were to wear gloves—the thin cotton kind that obscure fingerprints but don't kill tactile sensations. The transfer point to different cars was fixed fairly close by to facilitate our getting out of the hot car. And we would do the deed at night.

It felt good to have a solid plan, but that didn't mean there weren't complications. It was during this time that I had separated from my wife, Iris, and she was making things hard. After ten years of marriage, with a one-year separation between the sixth and seventh years, we just couldn't get to an understanding on anything, and with the urgent need I was feeling to engage in the struggle, I didn't really want to take time out to try. For me, the struggle took precedence over everything. It had been a century since blacks were "freed," but we were still the last hired and the first fired. And blacks were, and still are, the favorite targets of the racist police forces across the country. (It was a well-known fact that wherever the Ku Klux Klan was active, a large percentage of its members came from local police.) I knew that if someone didn't make the necessary sacrifice to try to set things right, it would never be done, and I wanted to be part of that change. Iris didn't approve of my political activities.

The real drama came when Iris told my comrades that I was in love with a white woman. She had found out about my relationship with Stephania and seized upon that to get sympathy from her friends and to sow discord between my comrades and me. At that time, in 1967, the concept of cultural black nationalism—the idea that black people should embrace only black culture and renounce anything to do with whites—was spreading like wildfire, and when one of my comrades asked me about Iris's declaration and then I confirmed it, he exploded. For him, anything white was bad. I just couldn't make him understand that it didn't change anything at all about me or my commitment to the cause. I told him that if for no other reason than my grandmother being white, I would not, could not ever hate all white people. I told him about Mark Hanson and how he had helped wake me up to the situation of blacks, and I told him of Nancy and Stephania, both of whom I had met at critical phases of my developing political consciousness. The only thing that counted for him was whether or not my loving a white woman would prevent me from going through with our planned action. If not, then he would see.

As it turned out, everything went as planned. The car was in place with the motor running, and the other comrade was in back holding the door open. For maximum steadiness, I placed the rifle on a log at the edge of the parking lot facing the station. I had a clear shot at a policeman seated at a desk near an open window. When I placed the crosshairs on him, another cop went out the door, got into a police car, and drove out of the park. I watched the car to make sure it wasn't coming our way, then relaxed a bit and canvassed the area again.

In a short while a police car entered the park and drove up to the station. I told my comrades to get ready, that this was it! It would be easier to get this one, out in the open, than the one behind the desk. It turned out to be the cop who had just left, and he got out of the car carrying something. Judging the distance and accounting for the drop of the bullet, I placed the crosshairs on his head, thinking I would hit him in the chest area. He turned from the car and started walking toward the station. I took a breath, let out half of it, started squeezing the trigger, and followed him with the crosshairs. About two or three yards from the door the rifle barked and belched out a flame that seemed to light up the whole area. I had never fired at night before, and I hadn't realized the importance of the flame that comes from a high-powered rifle. It blinded me. I didn't know if I had hit the target or not.

I sprang to my feet, dove into the car, and felt my comrade

pulling at me as he closed the door and the driver was burning rubber to get away. Everything went smoothly. We quickly changed into different cars and different clothing and then went our separate ways. I headed straight home and jumped in bed to try and calm myself and stop shaking. A big fat joint helped.

It was not until I woke up the next morning and turned on the news that I learned I had hit the target. The officer's leg was seriously damaged. I must have misjudged the distance; the drop of the bullet was more significant than I had allowed for, but the fact that he had been wounded gave me a sense of exaltation. Finally, I had returned a blow. I privately dedicated that one to the little black girls who were blown up in the church in Birmingham, Alabama. The feeling of cleansing was much as Frantz Fanon had described it in *The Wretched of the Earth.* For me, no matter what was to happen in the future, I would always carry the knowledge that I had struck a blow. I had proved to myself, through my action, that I really believed what I had been saying, that I wasn't just talk. I don't think I could have pulled the trigger if it had been otherwise. I was only thirty-one at the time, but from then on I could always carry my head high. True, that was only the beginning, but for me, the beginning was the most uncertain. Before, I didn't really know how I was going to react. But now I knew I had what it takes.

I dressed quickly to go buy the morning paper. The front-page article on our action was headlined MYSTERY PHANTOM SNIPER. I loved that. My only regret was that the satisfaction I was feeling had to remain a personal one. It couldn't be shared.

5

Use What You Got to Get What You Need

Before we entered into a direct relationship with the Panthers, our group had wanted to prove our worthiness by our actions. Since that was no longer in question, contact was made and a rendezvous fixed to meet at Huey's pad on Telegraph Avenue in Oakland.

I don't remember much about that first gathering. Other than meeting David Hilliard, the Panther party's chief of staff, for the first time, the only thing that stands out in my memory is a question from Huey as we were sipping coffee. He asked if I didn't think it better to be properly equipped before going into action; he suggested it was best to first rip off the necessary funds to get everything we needed in advance of launching a major effort. I had never anticipated such a question and wasn't prepared for it. I had practically memorized his essay "The Correct Handling of a Revolution," in which he spoke of teaching by example, and so I blurted out the first thing that came to mind, which was, "Use what you got to get what you need."

After the long, hot summer of 1967, with the rebellions in Newark, Detroit, and elsewhere, we felt that our preparations had, at least, put us on the same level as the rest of the country and that the revolution would not pass us by. Our San

Francisco group started attending and participating in any and all functions relevant to black people, and we tried to get to know everyone in our area associated with the struggle. We also continued our community meetings. News of the death of Che Guevara in October of that year had us walking around in a stupor for a while, and although that came as a severe blow to the international struggle for freedom and justice of all people, we were proud to be among those who had responded to his battle cry and had picked up his fallen arms.

Huey asked if we would conduct a meeting on Hunters Point for him. He was supposed to go, but something had come up and he couldn't make it. We were honored that he thought enough of us to ask, and we were more than enthusiastic to do whatever he wanted.

It was at that meeting that we had a new, surprising experience: we met our first resistance, in the form of Adam Rogers. He was supposed to have been the biggest, baddest nigger on Hunters Point, but when we encountered him, he came across like an Uncle Tom. He seemed to be impressed with our firearms demonstration, but he was violently against the idea of black people arming themselves for self-defense. He was convinced that would increase repression, even though history proved him wrong. When we examine the history of repression of black people, the only time there was a significant decline in police violence and murders perpetrated against blacks was precisely the period when blacks were organized and had access to guns. Given the wave of terror and violence against blacks that continues to sweep the country, I truly believe there is a lesson to be learned from that fact.

Rogers was one of the wounded in the Hunters Point rebellion of the year before, and a photograph of him had been used by the news media to illustrate articles on the riots that broke out following the killing of a black teenager by police that September. Because of that we were even more surprised by his reaction. It was not until later that we discovered that the administration of San Francisco mayor Joseph Alioto had sent in money after the rebellion and had bought off the so-called bad niggers. The same technique was used from coast to coast.

Despite Rogers, most everyone seemed to like what we had to say and really related to the firearms demonstration. Several people wanted to take courses in handling weapons, and so I fixed a rendezvous for the following Saturday at the parking lot of the abandoned shopping center right on top of Hunters Point.

The next day I arrived at the Point at seven in the morning, in order to get set up before people began to gather. There wasn't going to be any target practice, but I would be firing a few shots into the air by way of demonstration. I knew that would pose no problem as far as the police were concerned; due to their racism, whenever they heard shots on the Point, they generally looked the other way. Once, during a dispute between two gangs, shooting broke out and instead of the police coming in to break it up, they sealed off the area and let them shoot it out. The gun battle lasted twenty-four hours and the police didn't return until the next day.

At around eight o'clock I saw David Hilliard's car driving up, which I found surprising because we had only seen each other a couple of times before. As the car approached, I recognized Emory Douglas and George Murray. Everyone had strange looks on their faces that made it clear something was wrong. Damn! Huey had been shot and captured! He had shown up at David's, wounded and bleeding heavily.

There was real concern for his life, so David drove him to the hospital and left him on the steps, then drove straight to San Francisco to find me. He said Huey had asked him to ask *me* to help out with the aftermath—specifically dealing with the passenger who had been in Huey's car at the time of the shootout with Officer John Frey of the Oakland Police, who'd been killed. There was also the problem of the guns Huey had stockpiled. I'll never understand why David didn't just bring the guns with him, but he hadn't, and I was obliged to go back into the area, get everything, and get back out, safely. That might sound easy, but the shootout had occurred less than three hours before and there was one policeman dead and one seriously wounded. So, it was hot over in Oakland, to say the least.

There was no time to go by the house and unload the guns I had on hand for the training, so I followed David back to Oakland with a trunk full of weapons.

David took me into the backyard of a house that had a lot of weeds and a stack of old lumber in which he had stashed the gun. In his state of excitement he couldn't remember exactly where the pistol was, and while we were looking, an elderly black woman came out of the house next door and asked what we were doing. David kept searching and didn't look up. She then said, "If you don't come out of there I'm going to call the police." I began to panic and told David to say something to the woman. When he rose up, she recognized him and calmed down. This was David's house and she was his neighbor. On one hand, I was relieved, but on the other, if the police were looking for the passenger who had been with Huey, it was certain they wouldn't miss David's house, as both were known Panthers.

Finally, he found the gun. I took it and told him to get the passenger to a lawyer while I split back to San Francisco. That gun was the hottest thing I had ever had in my hands. It still had that inimitable odor of burnt gunpowder that lingers on a weapon after it has been fired. They say God looks after fools and idiots, and it must be so, as I made it back to San Francisco without incident.

I headed straight to the pad of a girlfriend who wasn't involved with any political activity in any form or fashion. I wanted to stash the gun at her house, but, bad luck, she wasn't home. I had recently met a sister named Barbara Easley who seemed cool, and as she lived close by, I went to her house. As soon as she opened the door, she asked if I had heard about Huey. I said yes and asked if I could stash something in her house. She agreed without hesitating, so I pulled out the pistol and stuck it under the water heater up among the pipes. Six months later, when we were moving Barbara's things to my pad (we had decided to live together), I reached up to make sure that the gun had been removed and was shocked to find the cylinder of the pistol, which also had the serial number of the weapon engraved on it. I didn't know who was supposed to have been responsible for removing the pistol shortly after it was put there, but all that time I had been staying with Barbara I was certain that it *had* been removed. That was my first real lesson in not depending on others, and I felt stupid that I had been confident enough to not even look to verify that it had been removed. To this day, I wonder whether or not that was incompetence or sabotage.

We all spent the day of the shooting practically in mourning. With one policeman dead, one seriously wounded, and Huey in their hands, we were all thinking the same thing, even though no one said it out loud: the gas chamber at San Quentin Prison. And that was if they didn't just kill him outright in the hospital.

A meeting was called at Emory's house to discuss Huey's case. There were no more than ten people, and we all agreed that we couldn't let Huey be sent to the gas chamber. The necessary machinery would have to be built to prevent it, and soon the Huey P. Newton Defense Committee was formed. It was at this same meeting that I first met Eldridge Cleaver. He was beginning to make contact with all of the political factions and tendencies in the Bay Area at that time. I attended a few gatherings, but some of the meetings got heated, with the various sides arguing over things that seemed, to me, to have no importance. I quickly grew frustrated and returned to our San Francisco group.

As for Huey, we knew we had to do something, quick. They had killed Malcolm, Che, Patrice Lumumba, and Mehdi Ben Barka, the Algerian leader, and now they were trying to kill Huey. We had to return blow for blow. From now on it was going to be an eye for an eye and a tooth for a tooth.

Meanwhile, my group of people committed to serious action had grown from three to six. Each of us submitted a proposal of what new action we might take, and the one adopted was a plan to attack the police station on Hunters Point. We had to move as fast as possible because if we allowed too much time to pass, the people would not make the connection between our action and the fact that the police had tried to kill Huey. We still had no propaganda machinery to get the word out.

We worked hard putting together and rehearsing the plan of attack and escape. Again, we put a lot of emphasis on the escape. We knew that anyone could do just about any action they wanted, but the key was to get away safely. The element of surprise is always crucial, and we would have to hope there had been no leaks and that our targets were not sitting there in ambush, waiting for us.

The night of the operation arrived and everything was ready. The getaway vehicle was in place with the motor running and the driver behind the wheel. One person was positioned to cover the back of the station with a twelve-gauge shotgun loaded with double-O buckshot in case any of the officers tried to escape by the back door. The rest of us were at the corner of the building, waiting in the shadows. I was in front and the air was thick with tension as I felt the eyes of the other comrades waiting for me to step around the corner, which would commence the operation. I made the step.

I passed the first window and a policeman looked out at me, but I was sure he couldn't see the guns because we were carrying them low. We were to begin shooting only when we were in position and had all the windows covered at the same time. If the shooting started before I reached the last window, those policemen inside might have the time to fire back. When the comrade behind me arrived at the first window and saw the policeman looking out, he shouted, "Motherfucker!" and started shooting. I ran as hard as I could to reach the last window and, much to my surprise, when I reached it the two policemen there were crawling on the floor to hide behind their desks. I started firing from the hip and nailed one to the floor. He happened to be a black policeman we knew from the year before because he'd shot a resident of the Fillmore District. An angry crowd had gathered and started to move on him, and in newspaper accounts of the incident, he had said that he was rescued by his "white police brothers."

We did not touch the other officer because we recognized him as the person who had rescued a black teenager who was being beaten by white policemen at the police station.

The whole operation lasted less than fifteen seconds and was a total success. We ran for the getaway vehicle, picked up the comrade watching the back door, and sped off. We arrived at the bottom of the Point before the first police car passed us going the other way, speeding up to the station. By the time roadblocks were set up, we had changed clothes and vehicles and were going our separate ways.

The next day, Adam Rogers and his followers set up a picket line outside of the station to denounce the attack and pledge their support to the police. It was unfortunate we didn't have a propaganda mechanism to deal with all that at the time, and looking back, that might have been our biggest error. We were waging war with the San Francisco Police Department, and although the score was two to nothing in our favor, it was primarily only them and us who knew about it. The only mention in the friendly press was a congratulations in the next issue of the Panther paper. Although we thought we were preparing to join black people waging war in the rest of the country, in reality we were waging a private war. We were not aware at the time that we were out on a limb by ourselves.

That December, the San Francisco Police became the first department in the country to create a special unit when they requested a budget to build barricades and fences and to install spotlights outside their stations, a way of protecting themselves from the guerrilla attacks perpetrated against them, they said. They were getting wise to us, but we had no plans to back down. Panther activities were also picking up steam. Eldridge was running around all over the place organizing people, trying to keep Huey out of the gas chamber, and I was still helping the San Francisco group organize when I wasn't working at my job every day. I was a respectable nigger by day and a guerrilla by night.

I was contacted by LaVerne Anderson, Huey's girlfriend, who set me up with Huey's lawyer, Beverly Axelrod, on the campus of the University of California at Berkeley. Beverly told me Huey wanted me to organize an escape for him. Words are hard to come by when I try to describe my feelings upon hearing that. It was a mixture of pride and joy on one hand—the pride and joy of knowing Huey placed enough confidence in me to make such a request—and, on the other hand, the new type of tension that was becoming familiar whenever I began work on a new operation. One of the strongest elements of that tension was fear.

There's no need to tell about all the planning we did to get Huey down from the eleventh floor of the Alameda County Jail to freedom; that would be a book in itself. What I will say is that it took a lot of people in addition to those who would actually carry out the operation, including Huey's brother, Melvin, who would deal with any funds needed, and of course Beverly, who had direct access to Huey and was naturally the linchpin upon whom the success or failure of the operation would depend. I can also say this: for all of you physical fitness fans, it is amazing what running up and down eleven floors of stairs several times a week will do for your physical condition—if it doesn't kill you.

In those first critical months of expanding the local group into a national organism moving under the name of the Black Panther Party, I was mostly just trying to figure out how to get Huey free. Because of that work and the need for utmost secrecy, I stayed only on the fringes of everything else. I did not take part at all in the day-to-day process of party decision-making, and I was even less involved in deciding future strategy. From the day Huey was shot in October of 1967 until January of 1969, I was not involved in the internal functioning of the party, which, in Huey's absence, had been turned over to Eldridge Cleaver and Bobby Seale.

6

Shake-'Em-Up

It was with enthusiasm and honor that we finally met Bobby Seale, the man who, with Huey, had cofounded the Black Panther Party in 1966. It was Bobby who had led the armed Panthers to the state capitol in Sacramento in May of 1967, and he was enthusiastic to meet us. Nothing was said directly, but he made it clear he had heard about our activities, and that swelled us with pride.

He asked if I would accept a position on the party's central committee. I was knocked off my feet, thrilled by the offer, and very proud. I had a nagging doubt about whether or not I was worthy of such an honor, but I told him I would submit the idea to our San Francisco group and abide by their decision. They had no objections, and I was overjoyed to accept. The only condition was that my appointment had to be kept a secret from those outside the inner circle in order to maintain my effectiveness within the group and my activities as a guerrilla.

By that time we had discovered Régis Debray's book *Revolution in the Revolution?*, which analyzed how small, determined armed groups could inspire and lead revolutions in Latin America; it reinforced our belief that armed action was the highest form of politics, and we didn't relate to any literature that didn't support that thesis. We also got our hands on General Võ Nguyên Giáp's *People's War, People's Army.* We had no doubt that the "foco" theory espoused by these leaders—in which a small group of individuals committed to revolution could lead by example and inspire a larger group—could be applied to the situation inside the United States. It was only necessary to adapt it to an urban situation.

Fueling our philosophy were incidents of violence against blacks. On February 8, 1968, three blacks were killed and fifty were wounded on the campus of South Carolina State University when highway patrol officers shot into the crowd during a demonstration protesting racial discrimination at a local bowling alley. Most of the protesters were students at the university and were gunned down by law enforcement including the local police, state troopers, and national guardsmen. Our anger grew.

A big rally was planned for February 25 to celebrate Huey's twenty-sixth birthday. It would be held at the Oakland Auditorium, and Stokely Carmichael would be coming. Many new members were recruited into the Panthers at that time, in part because it was necessary to increase forces to handle the workload, which was growing daily. I wasn't involved with planning the rally, but I did organize the security that was to be discretely placed throughout the auditorium. The Nation of Islam had killed Malcolm at a speaking event, so we wanted to be sure that if anyone attempted anything the night of the rally for Huey, we would be in a position to assure that, at the very least, he would not escape.

Few Panthers had handguns at that time. In discussing the problem with Eldridge, I told him that in Nevada it was possible to buy them over the counter like a pack of cigarettes, with no waiting as in California, where the police had to approve the purchase before a handgun was delivered. A few days before the rally Eldridge gave me two thousand dollars to make a trip to

Nevada and bring back a load of handguns.

In Reno I found an army surplus store that had a small counter where handguns were sold. The owner had just received a shipment of Astra 9mm semiautomatic Spanish pistols. I checked them out, saw they were in working condition, and told him I would take all that he had, pulling out a handful of crisp hundred-dollar bills. His eyes lit up. He brought out his wife and father from the back of the store to introduce them and made a pot of coffee. If it had been a century before, he probably would have been selling guns to the Indians, which was just what I was looking for; with the genocide of the Indians, the repressive machinery was now turned on blacks, so, in that sense, we were the Indians of today. He was only interested in money, and that suited me just fine. I told him to try to find some 9mm Brownings for me, and we exchanged telephone numbers. He said he would do his best, and I split back to San Francisco with my precious cargo.

The next day was full of anticipatory excitement. Stokely was the first to arrive. Eldridge, accompanied by a couple carloads of Panthers from Oakland, brought him to Barbara's house, where I was then staying, and then left to bring others. Eyes popped when I started passing out pistols. It was only a few hours before Huey's birthday rally, and thank God nothing happened at the rally that necessitated the use of weapons, because having put guns in the hands of people who had no training or practice, I'm sure it would have been a disaster. Stokely explained the difficulty they had on the East Coast acquiring handguns and convinced me to let him have some to take back. I couldn't help but be honored to be supplying Stokely Carmichael with guns, so I agreed and figured I'd just have to make another trip to Reno to replenish our supply sooner than planned.

When Eldridge returned, he was accompanied by none other than H. Rap Brown and James Forman. My head was swimming. Just a few weeks before, these were the people we were hearing about in the news and admiring the most for their militant activities, and now, here we were, all in the same room. It was really a surprise seeing Rap because he was supposed to have been under house arrest and not allowed to leave Manhattan.

In another car was Alprentice "Bunchy" Carter. After all I had heard about him as a founder of the Los Angeles chapter of the party, I was just as eager to meet him as the others. The thing that struck me about Bunchy was his eyes. He *looked* at you. It's rather difficult to articulate, but sometimes when someone is looking at you, you get the impression that their eyes aren't really looking at you—almost like a sideways glance—but when Bunchy turned his eyes on you, there was no doubt that he was really looking at you.

After everyone was assembled, we made a convoy and split for the Oakland Auditorium. Outwardly, the rally was a success. Eldridge announced the merger of SNCC and the Panthers, and also the appointment of Rap Brown as the party's minister of justice and James Forman as its minister of foreign affairs. There was also a lot of shit going on behind the scenes that I didn't understand. There were contradictions between Stokely, Rap, and Forman, both among themselves and between the three of them and Eldridge. And at the rally, Stokely spoke and completely contradicted everything he had said during his recent trip to Havana, Hanoi, and Europe. He more or less condemned all whites and any working coalitions with them, which was utterly contrary to the direction Eldridge had been taking the party in order to free Huey. According to what he had said earlier, it was necessary to make alliances wherever they could be made. The infrastructures available that would permit the necessary work of disseminating information were mainly in the hands of whites, and the idea was that whenever such resources could be found, and whenever those responsible were willing to put them at the disposal of the campaign to free Huey, there was nothing that would stop Eldridge from making an alliance.

After the rally Stokely decided to stay in the Bay Area for a few days more, which suited us fine. Our small group in San Francisco was convinced that if there was anyone who could tell us about and connect us to what was going on in the rest of the country, it was Stokely. For the past couple of years there had been no one who had commanded more attention from the media.

The day after the rally, before Rap and Forman left, everyone made the pilgrimage to see Huey in the Oakland jail. Pigs were everywhere. Even if you went to the toilet they were either already in there or they followed you in. And they were all over outside too. The street in front of Barbara's pad looked like the FBI's parking lot. When we moved in cars, they followed us, bumper to bumper. The heavy surveillance made us very uptight, to say the least. Stokely explained that, for him, it was always like that.

Invitations were coming in from all over the Bay Area for Stokely to speak, but he had agreed to meet our group at the first opportunity. I passed the word, and the reception for him was prepared. We went from meeting to meeting and finally, after two days and nights of constant activity, we were finally free and headed for the group rendezvous. When our convoy arrived, the neighborhood was so filled with supporters that the pigs had decided to move back and wait outside the area. The whole community had been alerted, and everyone came outside to see and talk to the great Stokely Carmichael. At the first opportunity, I pulled him away and led him down some stairs into a pitch-black basement. At the bottom, I raised a flashlight and moved it from face to face and made introductions. I then turned it on the long table that everyone was standing behind. I passed the light slowly from one end to the other. There were weapons of all types, ammunition, and a stack of dynamite and fuses, and spaced between the items were newspapers with headlines showing different actions we had carried out. Stokely's reaction shocked us. The nigger panicked and said, "Get me out of here."

Our admiration for his "militant" reputation did not let us believe what we were seeing. We attributed his reaction to the fact that only a few yards away were pigs of every species you could think of, and for him that meant danger. We were convinced that if he really knew this community and knew how it was organized, he would have felt as safe as he would have in his own home. We refused to consider the fact that he might just be all talk. Anyway, we asked him about the rest of the country and what was going on with other people moving in our fashion, but we didn't get a clear response. His visit ended up leaving us with more questions than answers.

Once we were past the excitement of the rally and its distinguished visitors, there was a meeting called of all the Panther leadership, which now included me. It was at that meeting, in March of 1968, when the definitive structure and hierarchy was outlined that was to govern the Black Panther Party until it cracked up in 1971. (The single change that took place during those years was the position of minister of education, originally held by George Murray. After Murray was jailed for making controversial statements while in his role as an instructor at San Francisco State College (now University), and then began claiming he was talking to God, he was replaced by Ray "Masai" Hewitt, from Los Angeles.) It was at that meeting that I was designated "Field Marshal."

Field Marshal! That sounded good. I knew of Field Marshal Bernard Montgomery of Britain and his reputation as an excellent strategist during the Second World War, and since I considered myself well on my way to a good military career, I thought the title of Field Marshal to be right in line. But, in terms of my work with the Panthers, I was hoping someone would tell me exactly what I was supposed to do. Sometime later I had the chance, or rather I took the opportunity, to ask Bobby Seale just what my responsibilities were. His response was not reassuring. He said simply, "Whenever you see something that needs to be done, do it."

The only clear-cut instruction I was ever given was to organize a Panther office in San Francisco. That was easy. It was only a matter of renting a storefront on Fillmore Street, cleaning it up, then painting and hanging out our shingle. At that stage in the development of the party, more people were coming to join than we had capacity to absorb. It was also at that time that I quit working my day job and became a full-time militant.

I rented a large five-room flat on Page Street so that my closest comrades wouldn't have any problems finding housing. Now when I would get up in the morning and step into the hallway, it would be wall-to-wall niggers. There was literally no place to walk. It soon became necessary to get other pads. Jerry Varnado of the San Francisco State Black Student Union took the flat next door, which was identical to the one I had just rented. Others took another flat around the corner. Finally, everyone had a place to sleep. Then the real work of learning to live together began. At the pad where I stayed, for example, the average number to eat and sleep every night was between forty and fifty. This experience in collective living was necessitated both by the struggle and by the need to provide for our own security. It also turned out that just the simple act of shopping for and preparing food was enough to revolutionize our way of thinking and doing things. We quickly found that individualism would block and destroy any incentives to do anything for the group; the only thing that worked was the subordination of one's own desires to the collective good. That may not sound difficult, but try doing it with dozens of people who don't know it's the only thing that will work—especially among males that had never spent one instant of reflection on the social relationships between men and women. Imagine taking junkies, dudes just out of the joint, and lumpen types from the ghetto and putting them in the kitchen to cook and clean up. I'll just say this: Whenever a pad was abandoned, for whatever reason, it was no longer fit for human habitation. You can't imagine the crap and filth created by forty to fifty people living together in five or six rooms; it was frightening. One day, I had to draw the line and call a meeting when it happened too many times in a row that I went to change my underwear only to find someone had taken my clean shorts. And that wasn't even the problem. The problem was that they were leaving behind their dirty ones. And they were dirtier than anything imaginable. To avoid an epidemic, I found it necessary to teach people basic hygiene.

Very quickly, individualism and selfishness became dirty words, and also liberalism. It was necessary to constantly give criticism and learn to make self-criticism. That's why Mao's teachings had such an influence on us. It was in his writings that we found principles to apply in learning to live with each other. It was the imperatives of the struggle that dictated the need for collective living and not any abstract idea about wanting to set up utopian communes.

In May of 1969 I left the Bay Area to go to the East Coast and put back together party chapters that had been severely damaged by the government's increasing repression. Two months later, I returned, just in time for the party's United Front Against Fascism gathering at the Oakland Auditorium—a kind of congress of antifascist organizations working for change.

When I walked into the Page Street pad where members of the group were living, my eyes watered up, but this time it was with tears of joy. Everything was neat as a pin, and everything was in its proper place. That reality represented a revolutionary change in the way my comrades had begun to live their daily lives with those around them. Their leap in consciousness, their level of respect for each other, meant that the day of victory was a little bit closer.

My other preoccupation during this time was military preparedness—specifically, assuring everyone had the necessary means of defense in case those cowboy pigs who parked in front of our houses and apartments every now and then with their shotguns hanging out the window got some ideas about playing Superman.

We had our neighborhood's security as well organized as was technically possible with what we were able to lay our hands on. All our pads were within a square block, and if anyone ever came under attack, there were several places to fall back on, each one organized as well as the other. Also in those first days there weren't yet rules within the organization that prevented anyone from setting up and executing on their own an unauthorized operation of a military nature. In fact, most ways that daily needs were provided for at that time could be classified as military. Nothing was ruled out. If it paid the rent, the gas and lights, the telephone, food, clothes, guns, ammunition, transportation, gasoline, office supplies, it was valuable.

In the year 1968, more arms were stolen from the mail in San Francisco than in the rest of the country combined. Being civil service work that required only a relatively simple test for employment, the personnel was about 80 percent black, and because the workers there made no contact with the public, they wore street clothes, making it easy for us to blend in. By way of pushing for gun control, someone in Congress got the brilliant idea to pass a law that required any package containing firearms to have a big red label on it saying "GUNS." We had a field day. Every now and then we would go down to the mail office, which was close to the Ferry Building, walk in through the loading ramps, which were never guarded, and pick up all packages with the red label—as simple as that. I don't know about the rest of the country, but I know for a fact that in San Francisco there were a lot of guns in niggers' hands.

Meanwhile, the task of preparing Huey's escape was nearing the stage of implementation. The target date—Easter Sunday—was about three weeks away, and our group had been working hard to ensure success. Security dictated that those of us involved in the effort remain on the fringe of other official party business, and that gave us a different perspective compared to what people closer to the action were experiencing. And we didn't like what we saw. It had become clear to us that the party leadership was running a heavy get-the-gun-and-do-your-thing line, but in reality we didn't see the rhetoric being put into action. We decided to invite the central committee for a meeting to let them know how we felt—and to pass on to them my most recent arms purchases.

Everyone showed except Bobby, since the pigs were looking for him. In addition to the central committee, there were several

East Bay Panthers, including June (Roosevelt) Hilliard, who was David's brother, and John Seale, who was Bobby's brother. The handful of us who had been working secretly for Huey's escape decided that, for just this one time, we would show ourselves as a group. By then we even had our own uniform, which was built on functionality rather than aesthetics: we dressed in all black and wore army field jackets that had good pockets for carrying things. Two comrades carried the two twelve-gauge riot pump shotguns I had bought, and the rest carried M1 .30-caliber carbines. After members of the central committee were seated, our SF group came out of a room where they had been waiting behind closed doors. No one knew they were there until they came in and positioned themselves across the room, facing everyone seated, with their weapons held across their chests.

We more or less told them we heard them talking and talking but didn't see them doing anything. We read quotes from Che and Mao on the necessity of example, plus another quote that went, "The primary job of the party is to provide leadership for the people. It must teach by words, and action, the correct strategic methods of prolonged resistance. When the people learn that it is no longer advantageous for them to resist by going into the streets in large numbers, and when they see the advantage in the activities of the guerrilla warfare method, they will quickly follow this example." We asked if anyone in the room knew the author of those words. David Hilliard was the only one who ventured a guess when he asked if it was Che. "No!" we said. "That was Huey P. Newton, your minister of defense, in his essay 'The Correct Handling of a Revolution.'" There were no visible reactions from the other side, but we had planted some invisible seeds. With that, we ended the meeting and gave them the arms we had been holding.

A couple of weeks later, on April 4, 1968, the Reverend Martin Luther King, Jr., was assassinated in Memphis, Tennessee. He was there supporting the garbage workers' strike. Black communities exploded, and 150 cities from coast to coast started burning. Our house immediately filled with people, armed to the teeth, asking, "What are we going to do?" It was with painful difficulty that I found the force to convince everyone that we had learned that unbridled violence was not the correct way to deal with such things. If anything was to be done, it would have to be planned and executed like a proper operation; there couldn't be any spontaneous stuff. It was even more difficult because I wanted to go out and do something myself.

After King's assassination, everyone lived in a state of constant alert. Security was reinforced all around, and weapons were constantly being cleaned and kept in readiness. By that time there was considerable interchange between the Panthers in Oakland and San Francisco. Wendell Wade and Li'l Bobby Hutton were among those who stayed with us for a few days. One evening was indelibly etched into my memory because it was the last time I was to see Li'l Bobby alive.

The evening after King's death, I received a phone call from Eldridge saying they were getting ready to move. I asked whether it would be on this side or that side, meaning in San Francisco or Oakland. He replied it would be on their side and hung up. I immediately alerted everyone, turned all our radios to different stations, and waited for news. I couldn't help but wonder why he had called to tell me. I wondered if he expected me to do something on my side of the bay and, if so, what? I just couldn't figure it out. We waited for the radio to give us some news, or for the telephone to ring.

It wasn't long before reports started coming in on the radio.

The first news flash spoke of a shootout in West Oakland, with several policemen wounded. Multiple arrests had been made, and reporters said shooting was still going on in the area. We immediately started making phone calls, and in record time we had organized teams of doctors and a couple of nurses that we either sent to a house in Oakland that was set up to receive the wounded or sent into the streets to rescue any stragglers that might be stranded in the area.

After it was all over, Li'l Bobby was dead and Eldridge was wounded and captured, along with eight others. What a catastrophe! Stragglers were picked up all over the place, and no two people had the same story. No one knew what had really happened. All everyone agreed on was that when the shooting began, niggers started running in all directions. And what was worse, in trying to escape and not be captured, they had thrown away their weapons. The police found guns all over the area. An impressive amount of equipment was lost.

Everyone loved Li'l Bobby. When he was shot down in cold blood after he'd surrendered to the police and come out of the surrounded house with his hands up, it was as if they had killed the soul of the Panthers. After Huey and Bobby created the party, Li'l Bobby became the first member. He was the party's treasurer, and he personified pride, courage, and revolutionary determination. During this final battle, he had stayed in the house filled with choking, blinding tear gas for an hour and a half, returning shot for shot with the pigs who had him surrounded. Li'l Bobby was seventeen years old, just two weeks shy of turning eighteen, when he was murdered.

Coincidently, Marlon Brando was staying with us at the time of the shootout. He had come up from Hollywood to get an understanding of what the Panthers were all about, and he stuck around for Li'l Bobby's funeral, which was attended by niggers from all over the Bay Area, the majority coming dressed in the Panther uniform—a black beret and black leather jacket. In paying last respects, everyone stood at attention, more or less in a military fashion. Also standing there was Brando. Naturally, a photographer seized the moment, capturing Brando standing with his hair blowing in the wind, a serious look on his face, with the military formation of Panthers receding into infinity in the background. Because of Brando, that photograph made the news and was published in magazines and newspapers around the world. It was that photograph that made the Panthers known on an international level for the first time. And that's to say nothing of the impact it had inside the United States. For many people across the country, this was the first time they had heard of the Panthers, and headquarters soon started receiving inquiries from all over the country on how to set up more chapters of the organization. The biggest impact the Panthers had on black people at that time was, finally, introducing the idea that there are niggers ready to fight back, in an organized fashion, with guns in hand.

But what a disaster! The only members of the central committee left on the streets that had been close to the day-to-day decision-making were Bobby Seale and Eldridge's wife, Kathleen. Everyone else was in jail, in the hospital, or dead. Nobody said it or showed it, but even though interest in the organization was up, the morale of the Panthers was at its lowest level.

As for the operation to bust Huey out, it was dead. The target date had been Easter Sunday, when the personnel of the jail would have been at its minimum, but that happened to be the Sunday after the shootout that cost the life of Li'l Bobby. All those busted in the shootout had been put into the same jail with Huey, and jailhouse security was reinforced, with policemen on every floor. Huey sent word to cancel the operation. Charles Garry, his lawyer, was confident that he could get Huey out of jail after a couple of years' work, and Huey was apparently ready to deal with it that way. Given the new situation, it was with relief that we received the order to cancel the operation.

With all the attention being drawn to the Panthers by then, the powers that be started intensifying their campaign of slander and denigration, using the examples of Huey's case, the shootout with Eldridge and Li'l Bobby, and the death of Bunchy's brother, Arthur "Glen" Morris, which had occurred the month before. In March of 1968, Arthur was the first Black Panther to be killed. It was Arthur who had introduced us to "shake-'em-up" (white port and lemon juice), and Arthur was the first one I heard use the expression "Right on!" Arthur had been set up for a rip-off in Los Angeles and received a twelve-gauge shotgun blast at point-blank range, although he was successful in shooting and killing his two assailants before he himself died. His death made only a small news item, but the shit hit the fan when the gun Arthur had used was traced back to the dealer in Reno I was doing business with.

When the authorities checked the dealer's books and saw all the guns I had been buying, they shit bricks. They used their flunkies in the press to run scare articles all over California. Every Bay Area newspaper carried front-page articles with headlines designed to alarm people, saying things like PANTHERS STOCKPILING GUNS. The articles went on to tell of my trips to Reno and the quantity of guns I had been buying. They left no stone unturned. They even went so far as to describe the money I was using, saying I was coming into the store with thousands of dollars of brand-new hundred-dollar bills. The fact that all my purchases were perfectly legal was omitted.

They did everything to frighten people and turn them against us. The California State Legislature also got into the act, and a bill was prepared making it illegal to purchase weapons out of state and then bring them back in. During the debate on the legislation, a colored assemblyman, Mervyn Dymally, read into the record the serial number of each gun I had purchased during my trips. I hoped he choked before he finished. There's nothing sadder than seeing a nigger Tom putting the noose around his own neck.

1

The Sky's the limit

All visible Panther activity was now directed toward getting Eldridge and the others released on bail so the work could be intensified to free Huey. At least all the attention the party was receiving had its positive side: it got the message out about Huey's case and the need for blacks to arm themselves for self-defense from coast to coast. At that time we did not have the organizational machinery to spread the word as far and wide as did the news articles designed to turn people away from us. Groups had begun forming all across the country, with people wearing black berets and black leather jackets calling themselves Black Panthers.

Since the dialectic is in all things, however, that new mobilization also had its bad side. It seemed each group of "Panthers" that had sprung up literally overnight had its own different ideology, and in many instances, irreparable damage was done that we were never able to correct because people were coming together under the name of the Black Panther Party but they had no idea what we stood for. It was even worse in Europe, where it seemed that every black who traveled abroad between 1968 and 1972 called themselves Panthers. Whenever real representatives showed up to organize some type of support activity, there were always a lot of difficulties to overcome caused by some jive niggers trying to get by.

We were not able to effectively move to clean that problem up until the spring of 1969. By then, with the help of supporters, everyone who had been busted in the shootout was finally bailed out. At the hearing for Eldridge, the state couldn't prove he had done anything, so he too was released. He was fortunate to have gone before a judge interested in justice rather than furthering his career. It was at that point the remobilization of the Free Huey campaign moved into high gear. Through a coalition between the Panthers and the Peace and Freedom Party, Eldridge became a candidate for president of the United States on the Peace and Freedom ticket. The party saw his candidacy as an effective way to make Huey's case known on the largest scale at that time, since as a presidential candidate, there were speaking engagements to be had in every corner of the country. That was the first big push of the Black Panther Party on a national scale, and wherever Eldridge went, teams accompanied him to handle organizational problems. If there was no party chapter in a particular location, they would set one up, and if there was one, they would clean it up, get it organized properly, and get the responsible leaders to headquarters in the Bay Area so they could find out what the Panther party really was. By election time of 1968, there were branches of the Panther party all across the country more or less coordinated from the headquarters in Oakland.

Eldridge made a memorable swing through the country. I recall the song he composed and that he convinced every audience to rise and sing with him at the end of every speech. At New York University, I even saw two nuns in their habits stand with the rest of the audience and sing "Fuck Ronald Reagan."

The best-known slogan that came from the Free Huey campaign was "Free Huey or the Sky's the Limit." People were organized from coast to coast around that slogan, and because of it, military preparations reached a fever pitch. We were always on the lookout to buy machine guns and hand grenades, but as far as rifles, shotguns, and handguns went, we really ended up with more than we needed. Our stocks of dynamite started growing also. When Huey's trial began on July 15, 1968, we were ready to implement that slogan.

A week later the central committee went to New York to present Huey's case to the United Nations. James Forman was to handle the arrangements of getting us into the UN and also setting up a press conference. That was in keeping with his title of minister of foreign affairs, and it helped that he already had observer status at the UN as SNCC's representative of international relations.

Money was collected and the entire central committee flew to New York. What a trip! When I traveled with Eldridge I usually dealt with his personal security, and therefore I was often in his company, which was an honor. We were picked up at the airport by members of the New York branch of the party, who put us in a rather beat-up car that was usually used as a gypsy cab. It didn't really matter to us, though; it was transportation that would get us where we needed to go. Three days later, however, we learned it was a stolen car. Those New York niggers were either crazy or double agents, we didn't know which. When twenty-one members of the local party were arrested less than a year later, in April of 1969, we learned that at least five police agents had been in leadership positions with the group and were responsible for the massive takedown of the group that came to be known as the Panther 21 or the New York 21. We also learned later that our bodyguards had been two women who worked for the department of corrections; they had been chosen as our bodyguards because they were the only members of the New York chapter who were legally authorized to carry guns. Man, they really did things different in New

York. I can only say that, having just left a community where military preparedness and precision was the order of the day, the differences in the party from California to New York were radical, if not revolutionary.

Eldridge and I stayed at the home of our bodyguards. That was the first occasion we had time alone to talk since the first meeting after Huey had been shot, and I finally had the chance to ask him if the meeting our group had called to criticize the central committee had prompted the action in which Li'l Bobby was killed and Eldridge himself was wounded and captured. I wasn't really surprised when he said yes. I wanted to know how it had happened; it didn't appear to me that the planning of the operation had been very thorough. I couldn't believe my ears when he said the only plan was to go find some pigs. No organization, no rehearsal, nothing. Just a haphazard assemblage of niggers who were handed guns and told, "Let's go." In addition to that, one of their group had just shot up some drugs. No one else knew it at the time, and Eldridge told me that this individual not only talked after he was arrested but he told the truth, and then embellished on it. Now, I knew that when it came to political affairs Eldridge had no equal at the time, but when it came to handling the military side of Panther actions, something was obviously not working. So I told him that, from then on, if there was anything he needed done of a military nature, he was to call on me and I would deal with it for him.

By the time we got to New York, the internal contradictions in SNCC were at an all-time high, and to top that off, it seemed that James Forman was going into a nervous depression. Not only had he not made the arrangements to get us into the United Nations, but his press conference didn't come off right either. So there was the entire central committee of the Black Panther Party displaced for nothing. Talk about some mad niggers! And everyone was packing heavy. The lid was just barely held on when that all went down. When we finally got into the UN, it turned out to be only a symbolic gesture, a matter of "being received" by someone—I don't remember who—who could do no more than take the dossiers we had brought stating Huey's case and see that they were distributed to UN delegates. At the press conference, there was more sabotage, as it seems the press was told it would be happening at one time and we were given another. A real fiasco.

Among the New York Panthers who stood out and made an impression on me, two of the best were Sekou Odinga and Lumumba Shakur. These were some right-on brothers. They turned me on to my very first hashish. There was also Janis; Zayd Malik Shakur, the minister of information in the Bronx; and Chairman Brothers. It was clearly due to shortcomings on my part, but I could never reconcile the image of Chairman Brothers, looking like a Sunday school teacher, being an official of the Black Panther Party. I know looks are only superficial and it's what's inside that counts, but every time I saw Chairman Brothers I wanted to offer him a seat or something.

The policemen in New York were a little different too. The day we went to the UN there was a simultaneous street march with hundreds of Panthers from the New York area plus around two thousand supporters mobilized from the community. I remember seeing all those blacks coming down the street waving those blue flags with the Panther emblem and the demand to "Free Huey." Those of us who were to go inside were gathered on the corner across from the UN building when a New York City policeman came up to me and said, with a thick foreign accent, "It's against the law for more than three of you to be assembled at one time." I was so taken aback by the ridiculousness of what he said that all I could do was laugh.

But it was sad evidence of the state of American society that a white, foreign-born citizen who spoke broken English could shoot me down and be acquitted for justifiable homicide the next day. Me, who was still fighting for the freedoms that my grandfather didn't get over a century ago when he was released from the Cox plantation.

Stokely had come to New York to go to the UN with us, and after everything was over he asked me to accompany him on a speaking trip to Mobile, Alabama. I was enthused at the prospect of finally seeing the South. I talked it over with Eldridge, then accompanied Stokely to his pad in Washington, D.C. The thing that always bothered me about being in Stokely's company was the constant surveillance; you literally couldn't do anything without the authorities right there under your nose, and I could never get used to that. At least in California they respected us enough to keep a certain minimum distance, but with Stokely it was ridiculous. Our last day in Mobile the agents called us in the morning to wake us up so that we wouldn't miss our plane.

Traveling in the South with Stokely was an eye-opener. Black people loved Stokely. Wherever we went they came from all around to see and cheer him. Young, old, crippled, blind, everybody. That was one of the biggest differences I saw between the North and the South. In the North it was the youth, but in the South it was everybody who was mobilized.

From Washington to Mobile there was a layover in Atlanta, and that was also a revelation for me. It was the first time I ever saw black people living like white folks. Of course there were the poor parts of town, as in any other city, but that was the first time I saw whole sections of town occupied by blacks as bourgeois as anything I had ever seen. I was very surprised.

The arrival at the airport in Mobile was yet another new

experience. Everyone turned out in force to welcome Stokely. There were black people, but also plainclothes agents, local police, and FBI everywhere. Mobile was the first city in the Deep South I had seen, and the surprise for me was the fact that there were two distinct worlds, one black and one white, even down to the styles of the buildings. It looked like a place where one could live without ever having to go downtown and mix with white people. Out in the community, there was a festive atmosphere surrounding Stokely's visit. Everybody wanted to see the brother, and everybody wanted to feed us. I had some memorable baked shrimp and unforgettable steaks in Mobile.

Wherever we went, Stokely would introduce me as the Field Marshal from California. During our stay a group of people organized a meeting to ask about things on the West Coast, but they didn't want to hear any talk about politics. They wanted action. They wanted to know what we were going to do and when we were going do it. I learned in Mobile that you don't mobilize people if you're not serious, because they will call your hand every time.

Huey's trial ended on September 9, 1968, and at last the day of the verdict arrived. He was convicted of voluntary manslaughter in the death of Officer Frey and sentenced to two to fifteen years in prison. At the San Francisco Panther office so many people gathered to protest that they couldn't all get inside, and by the end of the afternoon the street was practically blocked. The tension in the air was heavy. Everyone was waiting for the call to action from headquarters. Frankly, by that time I understood that no such word could—or would—be given. The April shootout when Li'l Bobby was killed was the best illustration of what happens when things were done in that kind of haphazard manner. I was thankful that it wasn't on me to take the first step.

Time passed with no action, and eventually we reached a point when everyone in the San Francisco group thought it best that I take the initiative to call headquarters and see what was going on. Bobby came to the phone and explained, in a calm and logical way, that "Free Huey or the Sky's the Limit" was our organizing slogan, implying it would guide what came next. I understood and agreed with most everything he said. I also understood that you don't mobilize people around a slogan of action if you never intend to follow through with it. The masses alone, without the guidance of an organization, might not have the capability to analyze a situation and devise a strategy and action efficient enough to deal with it, but when they give their confidence and support to those that have the audacity to do so, their intelligence and understanding must constantly be respected and nurtured. I don't know of a more invincible weapon than honesty.

True enough, standing before me were hundreds of people ready to implement the slogan that had been invoked if Huey was not freed. And he hadn't been. Charles Garry was confident he could have Huey on the streets with a couple of years' work, and it would turn out that he was right, but, at the time, it was on me to hang up the phone, turn to the waiting crowd, and convince them of all that. I was ashamed and embarrassed, and I wanted to run and hide. It was all so dishonest to have sworn action and then be doing nothing. I was wondering what would be left after I finished talking. I was convinced that the Panthers would now be considered part of the crowd of "all talk and no action."

After the Huey verdict, attention slowly changed focus to Eldridge's case. He had been accused of attempted murder during the Oakland shootout. He had been released on bail, but when he went to a later hearing, he was ordered back to prison to serve the rest of the sentence. He had around four or five years left to serve. For the time being, however, he remained out on parole.

On my last trip to Reno, I'd been informed by the arms dealer that he couldn't sell me anything, but he also told me that the FBI had rooms at the hotel around the corner and he was supposed to call them the instant he saw me. I realized that to stay in business he would have to do their bidding, but I also began to think that behind his desire for money he might have other, more positive qualities. He could have sold me the guns, called the FBI, and lost nothing, but instead he told me that, as far as he was concerned, I had the right to buy as many guns as I wanted, just like anyone else. He said if I had brought someone with me, he would sell the guns to them and technically be in the clear. That was perfect, and after carrying out that plan and buying everything he had, I took only back roads to get to the Bay Area in case the FBI had had the store under surveillance. I was driving my GTO and was prepared to give them a run for their money.

With the loss of our Reno connection, we needed a new supplier, and soon we discovered the army surplus store at 85th and Western in Los Angeles, which had a big gun department. I dressed as a businessman and flew down to purchase fifteen Tanker-model M1 rifles. I went to fellow Panthers Ericka and John Huggins's pad to prepare for the trip back to San Francisco. Captain Franco (Frank Diggs) was there, and the three of them helped strip the cases of all identification and then drove me to the airport. The airline didn't want to let me on the plane with all those packages and said I would have to send them air freight. I convinced them that the cases contained flags that were needed urgently in San Francisco for a convention, and with a five-dollar bill to each of the airline workers, they were loaded on the plane with me.

That was one of the closest times I came to being busted. Apparently, after I had made the purchase, the people at the army surplus store had called the FBI and while I was flying to San Francisco the person in the car that had driven me around in Los Angeles was vamped on by the local police and FBI agents. I didn't know it at the time, but it was illegal to have in your possession more than nine weapons of the same type and caliber. The law said that constituted an arsenal and was a felony offense.

John called Panther headquarters to have someone pick me up at the San Francisco airport. After getting off the plane, I got a porter with a trolley, loaded up the fifteen cases, and with as cool an air as possible, headed for the exit. When I reached it I almost fainted. Someone at headquarters had sent five of the baddest, meanest-looking Panthers, in uniform, to meet me. I told them to get the stuff into the car, quick, and let's get out of here! If there were any agents around at all, either local or federal, they would have recognized the telltale silhouette of the gun cases and would know what was inside. I must say that there is such a thing as luck. The next day I received a phone call at the San Francisco office saying, "Hello, Donald, this is the FBI and we would like to know what you plan to do with all those guns." I never quite figured out if the agents were obliged by Hoover to make such stupid phone calls, or whether they thought I might really tell them something, or whether they were messing with me just to have a good laugh.

Eldridge was traveling all the time then. The election was just a few weeks away. I was impressed with his "gift for gab" and how he could convince any audience to listen to his words and sing his song. But I also saw a certain type of history repeating itself. Everywhere he spoke at that time he said that when the day came when he was to surrender and go back to prison, he would barricade himself deep in the black community, in Oakland, California, armed to the teeth and surrounded by Panthers. And, if the authorities wanted him, they would have to shoot their way in to get him. Now, that sounded bad and always got some cheers, but really, I knew that he knew that this wasn't really the way to deal with that possibility. And yet even after the shootout when Li'l Bobby was killed, there was the nagging question of whether or not he would try something like that. That question wasn't answered until the last time I saw him in the States and he admitted the situation couldn't be dealt with that way and that instead of staying and fighting he would be splitting. When we said our goodbyes, we embraced, not knowing when we'd meet next. I didn't see him again until the following year, when I visited Algiers, on the north coast of Africa, where he would ultimately end up after dodging his parole hearing.

Stokely, meanwhile, was also doing a lot of traveling and speaking. He had a letter from the people in Mobile, Alabama, requesting that I come down and teach them a few things, and since he had a speaking trip lined up already, it was agreed that I would accompany him and afterward go on down to Mobile and see what I could do. Stokely and I went everywhere: Detroit, St. Louis, Boston, Chicago, and many places in between. We then went to his pad in Washington, D.C., to rest up before the trip south. In our private discussions we were trying to reach an agreement on how we were seeing things, and in the end we had to agree to disagree. I was—and remained—convinced that any meaningful change in the situation of black people in the United States was intertwined with meaningful change for everybody. The present form of racism keeps people with common economic interests divided and at each other's throats, and I knew one thing for sure: If the American people could be made to realize that everyone is a victim of the present social and economic order, instead of following the finger pointing at blacks, or at Arabs with their oil, there could be effective mobilization and change inside the United States. Stokely, on the other hand, believed that the only solution was to "kill them all." The whites had to die. Between us, his nickname became Kill-'em-all Carmichael. I remained firmly convinced that we needed to learn to live with each other or face certain extinction—for the entire human species and maybe all life forms.

As a result of my observations during my travels, I slowly began to realize that the direction our group had been moving was far in advance of the rest of the country. I found nothing, anywhere, on the same level. I began to see why we hadn't gotten a clear-cut answer from Stokely when we asked him what was going on in the rest of the country, and I began to see, thanks to my travels with him, that the present need was to elevate the consciousness of people to the point that they would not only support but join in on the type of activities we had been engaging in as a smaller group. The objective conditions were ripe—in fact, they were rotten—but unfortunately the subjective conditions were nowhere near ready to begin moving the rest of the country the way we had been moving.

We left Washington, D.C., and headed for Atlanta, stopping at every major city for speaking engagements. The enthusiasm I saw was rather frightening—frightening because I wasn't seeing evidence that we were capable of properly organizing the people and raising them to a higher level of consciousness. The most frightening realization of all was that the people were expecting us to.

In Atlanta I took my leave of Stokely and headed for Mobile. I was surprised to see that the agents who usually followed

Stokley around were now just as interested in me, and I too had a welcoming party at the airport. That was going to be a problem. I wasn't there on a speaking trip, I was there to work, and I couldn't do that if the authorities were on my tail. So I had to hide out for three days before they got confused enough to start looking for me somewhere other than the last place they had seen me.

When I was finally able to see the people who had asked me to come to Mobile, they wanted to know what was going on in the rest of the country and which way the Black Panther Party was going. I relayed my own ideas (which turned out to be wishful thinking on my part), and then they were ready to get down to more serious business. By then I was sure of one thing: One was not supposed to encourage people to take a path that one was not sure about. I talked to them of the need to be organized and have confidence in one another, and I thought a good way to build the necessary unity of a group was by starting out with simple things and then moving on to more complex projects as confidence and unity was built. As for sharing practical information, I showed them how to make a Molotov cocktail that doesn't have to be lit but explodes into flame upon impact.

After the sessions ended I started circulating freely, and boy, were the agents glad to see me. That time they stuck to me like white on rice as I spent the next few days moving around meeting groups all over town. The people of Mobile left me with some indelible souvenirs, and I remember them as just about the warmest, most welcoming people I had ever met.

One evening while hanging out at my favorite club, round about midnight, one of the people I had come to see showed up with a big grin on his face and told me to come outside, as he had something to show me. As I stepped out of the door I froze in my tracks. I knew immediately that my visit to Mobile was over. The sky was red. It looked like half the town was burning. Needless to say, I got out. About a month and a half later, I received a package from Mobile that was full of newspaper articles about the incident. It seems that my visit had inspired more than one hundred fires, resulting in millions of dollars in damage. I knew I wouldn't be able to visit Mobile again anytime soon.

It was the end of 1968, and Richard Nixon had been elected and Eldridge had disappeared. I went back to Washington and then on to New York to spend a few days with Stokely and his family. He had anticipated Nixon's victory and had already made plans to leave the country at the first of the year, which was about a week away. We said our goodbyes and I returned to California.

8

Repression

I WAS NOW CONVINCED that the priority was to work in the communities to increase the people's consciousness. Any actual fighting in the war of liberation would have to wait.

I arrived back in San Francisco in the middle of a crisis: the entire San Francisco chapter of the Black Panthers had resigned. That was in January of 1969. During my absence, the decision-makers at the Oakland headquarters had created an internal police force, the "black guard," and its first act was to go to San Francisco to try to intimidate everyone and bring them under headquarters' direct control. To understand the full impact of what had happened, it is worth knowing certain characteristics about the people in our San Francisco group: We never sought personal glory or attention. We never engaged in power struggles or anything like that. We considered unity and love vital ingredients of any successful struggle. Every move we made was in the interest of the struggle, or so we thought. The party leadership, however, wasn't always on the same page.

One incident that highlights the discord between the factions happened on the night of a rally at the Fillmore Auditorium. Bobby Seale came over with a carload of Panthers from Oakland, plus a few bottles of Scotch. That not only surprised us but was cause for concern among the San Francisco Panthers because one of the requirements for being a member of the organization was following all the rules and regulations. Rule number three stated that no Panther was to be drinking while doing party work, and rule number seven stated that no member of the party was to be armed while under the effects of alcohol or drugs. Nothing was said at the time because of the respect everyone had for Bobby, but we all felt that he was showing a bad example and that he seemed to be establishing a double standard: do what I say, not what I do. He and those who had come with him hit the Scotch pretty heavy that night, and sometime over the course of the evening, one of the people with him—a man no one knew—pulled out a gun. Luckily, we never found out what he intended to do with it because the instant he came out with it he was pinned to the floor, thanks to the quick action of our security people. Instead of being commended for their vigilance, however, they were condemned—by Bobby! That was a flagrant injustice, clear to everyone. The next thing we knew, the black guard had shown up, ordered me to turn over the security guard to them, confiscated his weapon (which Eldridge had bought), and then proceeded to beat him as punishment for his vigilance.

With incidents like that having escalated the tension, I arrived back in San Francisco just in time to avert what surely would have been a bloodbath. After much discussion, things were kept under control, but the idea that the Panthers should have an internal police force like the black guard drove away more than one good militant at that time. For those of us who stayed, we considered it an unfortunate incident and a reminder that we would all do our best to ensure it never happened again. Unfortunately, as far as the San Francisco group was concerned, the seeds of mistrust between the militants at the base and the party leadership at the top had been sown.

Soon after that, I was summoned to a meeting of the central

committee, which by now was really thinned out. Bobby and David Hilliard, the chief of staff, did most of the talking, and what it boiled down to was them telling me I no longer had the right to travel without their authorization. No consideration at all was given to the fact that my travels had been done with Eldridge's knowledge and consent. I was convinced that meeting was in retaliation for the incident at the Fillmore Auditorium; they wanted to remind our San Francisco group that the Oakland leaders were still in charge. David asked why I hadn't been there when it was time to barricade ourselves with Eldridge, basically questioning my commitment to the party. When I said Eldridge had told me he wasn't going to do that because he intended to split, he seemed surprised and said no more. The meeting ended with a threat: I would be killed if I went running around again without their permission.

My head was swimming. Just two days before I'd had a meeting with Bobby and David in which I'd told them of my travels and my assessment of the situation on a national scale, and of my belief that it was now necessary to redouble our efforts on the community level. And now my love and admiration for the Panthers and my renewed dedication, coming as a result of my travels, had only brought threats on my life. I was so upset I couldn't reason. I assumed there had to be a misunderstanding somewhere and all I had to do was figure out what it was and then everything would be all right.

By January of 1969 the Black Panther Party had chapters all over the country. The party, as it then stood, had been built up by Eldridge (with the help of countless thousands, naturally) to keep Huey from being sent to the gas chamber. Huey was then in prison at the California Men's Colony in San Luis Obispo, California, and Eldridge had fled the country and gone into exile. None of us who were left really knew what to do.

Other than the campaign to free Huey, there was no long-range strategy or plan of action for leading the struggle, despite the fact that we now had a national organization in our hands. We hit the books to grasp Marxism-Leninism as a tool that would help us with the task ahead, and political education became the order of the day. Daily community work continued, but every spare minute was used to study. Each branch was to conduct at least three formal political education classes a week, and in addition to attending classes at the branch offices across the Bay Area, we all went to headquarters on Sundays for a general class. The demographic makeup of the organization was such that there were many members who could not read or effectively understand what they were reading, and so we used the tried-and-true method of going through the materials word by word, line by line, not advancing until everything was understood by all.

Ironically, the ideological basis for the internal destruction of the Black Panther Party was laid with the first book we studied. It was Joseph Stalin's *The Foundations of Leninism.* That text was used to instill love for the party above everything else—even, eventually, the struggle, as it turned out. We didn't know then that Stalin had massacred millions in the name of the party, and I must admit that, at the time, I'm not sure it would have mattered. That thought is very frightening, but it is one I cannot deny. One thing proved certain: if you can get an African American lumpenproletariat to love Stalin, you either have a true revolutionary or a cold-blooded killing machine.

As the ideas of Marxism-Leninism spread throughout the party, it quickly became afflicted with avant-gardism and elitism, considering itself the sole possessor of the truth. Anyone who didn't adhere to Marxist-Leninist ideas was treated as an inferior being, worthy of being despised. Adopting the Marxist-

Leninist structure of the party, with democratic centralism as its soul, all power was then confiscated in the name of the central committee, which, in reality, meant just David and Bobby. In name I was a member of the central committee from the time I met Bobby at the beginning of 1968 until I resigned in the autumn of 1972, and during that time there was never one meeting of the central committee, nor were there ever points at which members of the central committee were asked to vote on any proposition. Or, if there was, I was never told about it. Whenever David or Bobby thought up anything, it was simply sent down through the organization as a directive from the central committee. Frankly, I did not object to that way of doing things at the time because I didn't know what else to do. I was aware of my intellectual limitations and had no pretentions of being a political analyst, so I blindly went along with the usurpation of power, as did most everyone in the party at that time.

In the beginning of 1969 it also became necessary to clean up the organization and instill discipline. For the mobilization of the Free Huey campaign, recruitment had been wide open, and not much more than loyalty was asked of our members. As long as one did what one was told, that was about all that was required to be part of the party. As a consequence, there were many undisciplined individuals claiming the Panther title. Many "Panthers" would only show up at rallies or events where they got the opportunity to look sharp in the Panther uniform, but when it came to everyday work like selling papers or distributing leaflets, they thought that was beneath them. Some related only to the uniform and the gun. With the lull in "floor show" activities after Huey was imprisoned and Eldridge was in exile, these individuals began roaming around intimidating people, trying to prove how bad they were. That, combined with some being caught in petty robberies, started heaping scorn on the reputation of the party, and eventually someone decided it was necessary to begin purging the membership of all uncontrollable elements. And the axe started swinging. I believe it was necessary; there were some righteous fools, dangerous in their stupidity, who, if left unchecked, would have destroyed the party in short order. Expulsion notices were published weekly in the party newspaper, and in addition to the purge, a new rule was imposed to stop all the petty criminal activity that was tarnishing the party image. Henceforth, any operations of a military nature had to be approved by the central committee.

Operating with the personal authorization of Huey, I had organized and was working with several groups outside the formal party structure. The requirement from Huey was that they all had to adhere to party rules and regulations and accept the Panther philosophy. Not one of those groups had ever been involved in a mishap; no one ever got busted carrying out an operation, and all operations had been deemed successful. These groups were strong, disciplined, and proud.

When I passed on word of the new rules to one of the groups, however, there was a very negative reaction. It was, more or less, "Fuck the central committee." Again, I blocked. I talked of the need to stay in the party because of the level of work that needed to be done. The party had to be strengthened to be able to deal with the task ahead. I wasn't ready to leave the party personally, and since I was staying, I was going to abide by the rules and regulations. The thing that made the negotiations difficult for me was the fact that the new rules would necessarily shut down an operation we had been working on that would have been beneficial to everyone. It was planned for the very weekend after the new rules were made, and we didn't want to abandon it. After some discussion, members of this group agreed that I would ask the central committee for authorization to carry out the operation anyway. I had a meeting with Bobby and David on a Friday night to tell them of our plan. They said we would have to ask Huey and then do whatever he said. I contacted the group and relayed the response.

Early the next morning, to my surprise, someone from the group came by and woke me up to tell me they didn't want to wait to see what Huey said and had gone ahead and gotten a replacement for me so they could proceed with the operation as planned. I was told there was nothing to discuss. There was nothing for me to do then but sit back and let it happen. Since I knew all about the operation, I knew precisely what time it was supposed to jump off, so I turned on the radio and waited. It was a very punctual operation, and news flashes came just minutes after the operation was put into motion. But something had gone wrong: one person had been arrested. He was my replacement. I drove straight to Oakland, feeling it was necessary to warn headquarters in case the action was able to be connected to the party. I did it prepared to suffer the consequences. Since I had just been told the night before to wait for Huey's decision, I was expecting to, at the least, be expelled. To decide my case, a quick meeting was called of all the leadership present, including Bunchy Carter, founder of the Southern California chapter. The final decision was that if the operation turned bad for the party, I would be expelled. If it didn't, I had to leave the San Francisco office and report to Oakland headquarters every day instead. The thing that bothered me most was having Bunchy look at me when I was leaving and say softly, "Some people think they're special."

Well, the leadership had been wanting control of the San Francisco office, and now they had it. The operation did not turn bad, so instead of being expelled I would be punished.

I would now have to go to headquarters every day; my wings were clipped. We all knew I was being disciplined not because of the operation, per se, but because I had known that it was going ahead anyway and hadn't immediately reported that information to headquarters. I was being punished because I showed more loyalty to my comrades and the cause than to the party leadership.

The party then received its biggest shock since Li'l Bobby was killed. Bunchy and John Huggins were shot down on the UCLA campus by members of the cultural nationalist group called the US Organization, headed by bald-headed Ron Karenga. We were in a bitter fight with Karenga and had condemned what we called "pork-chop cultural nationalism." We didn't think there was any such thing as a cultural revolution divorced from armed struggle or class warfare. As the party newspaper put it in the issue of March 16, 1969, we accused Karenga and his ilk of being "the champion of the status-quo and articulating a sensational, comical racism as a cover-up for counterrevolutionary politics and concrete economic issues." We went further, accusing cultural nationalism as being "loved dearly by the racist pigs of the power structure because it divides the oppressed and exploited workers on the basis of skin on the one hand and acts as the seed bed for Black Capitalism on the other." Bunchy and John were killed just shy of a year after the death of Arthur, Bunchy's brother, the first Black Panther to be killed. That hurt real bad. Up until then, the Panthers' struggle against cultural nationalism had been on an ideological level, but now it was war. Anyone in the party who had ever had contact with one of these cultural groups—which was practically everybody—was now suspect. It was open season on niggers with bald heads, which was a popular style for followers of nationalist philosophies. I'm sure some Los

Angeles barbers lost some business around this time.

I was designated to go down and deal with the Los Angeles office after attending Bunchy's and John's funerals. This assignment was given in such a way that I could not help feeling it was intended to put me in the hot seat. And it was hot. Niggers with bald heads were looking to shoot at anything in a black leather jacket, and niggers in black leather jackets were looking to shoot at anything with a bald head. When you war with the police, they come into your area as strangers, but when you're warring with people from your own community, it's much more tense because you both know the same terrain. I don't know the exact number of deaths that resulted from the war of attrition that followed, but I think it was around six. I was glad to get back to the Bay Area, where things were calmer.

In response to the killings, all resources of the Black Panther Party were mobilized, from coast to coast, in condemnation of cultural nationalism. Later, when the COINTELPRO efforts were exposed in 1971, it became clear that the FBI had been right in the middle of it all, pitting groups against each other in an effort to neutralize various efforts to empower blacks. The other notable point of interference from the authorities was of course the April 1969 indictments of twenty-one Panthers from the New York chapter who were charged with conspiracy in the plan to attack several police stations. Their bail was set at $100,000. It was immediately clear that the operation had been the work of police agents embedded inside the party, and even though all of the Panthers were eventually acquitted, we then found ourselves looking out not just for niggers with bald heads but for agents and provocateurs who said they were on our side.

Kathleen Cleaver, who had stayed behind when Eldridge fled the country, was supposed to speak at an antiwar rally in Central Park, but at the last minute the central committee decided to send me instead. I was now convinced that every time there was trouble or risk involved, I would be chosen to represent the party. That was okay with me—at least I would be traveling again.

But it was a joke sending me to make a speech. I had never done that before and was scared to death. My work to that point had been such that it was necessary for me to keep as low a profile as possible and stay away from the limelight, so I hadn't had any experience speaking before large crowds. Being as uptight as I was, I knew I couldn't deal with it. The only solution was to use the six-hour plane ride to write a statement to read, rather than rely on any ability to speak off the top of my head. It was a good thing I did that, because when I arrived at Sheep Meadow in Central Park, there were what seemed like five hundred thousand people there. It was unimaginable. In addition to all the people in the crowd, it was wall-to-wall pigs. Up until that time, whenever I had been at a public event, security had always been provided by the organizers of the event, which meant they were sympathetic to the cause, but there in Central Park, security was composed of policemen in uniform standing shoulder to shoulder all along the edge of the stage. I couldn't think of anything more ridiculous than police acting as security. It was difficult, to say the least, getting used to the way they did things in New York. I swallowed my heart, got up on stage, read the statement I had written, and quickly got out of there.

Upon my return to headquarters, the leadership decided that it was an urgent necessity to send people to every corner of the country where there were groups operating in the name of the Black Panther Party. On adopting the Marxist-Leninist model of the party, as defined by Stalin, the party was then governed, in principle, by democratic centralism, which meant all branches were now required to adhere to the party line and to discipline as defined by the central committee. Branches that did not follow this rule were to be dissolved as necessary. Representatives were sent out across the country to give coherence to the mass that was moving in the name of the Black Panther Party, and where branches could be saved, their leadership was sent to headquarters to receive intensive, firsthand political education and observe how the party functioned on the West Coast.

For the first time in months, I was allowed to spend time again in the San Francisco office, this time to prepare for mobilization in advance of a rally to be held on May Day in front of the Federal Building in San Francisco. Everyone worked hard putting up posters and passing out leaflets to ensure the success of the rally, but we ran into trouble one day when one Leroy Looper got upset and said a comrade couldn't put up posters outside Looper's center for drug addicts, which had opened a couple of doors down from the Panther office on Fillmore Street. We don't know what the comrade told Looper, but Looper came to the Panther office with a gun and emptied it inside. Fortunately, no one was hit, but that man had to be insane. I rushed from my home, which was only a few blocks away, formed an execution squad and, arms in hand, combed the Fillmore looking for Looper. As far as we were concerned, anybody who would shoot up a Panther office had passed his own judgment. We weren't going to disappoint all the people in the area who had witnessed his stupid act and who were standing around watching to see what we were going to do. It was going to be a public execution in the middle of the street for everyone to see. Fortunately, we didn't find him. After that incident, we put guns in the office in case anyone ever had such ideas again.

As May Day drew near, we increased our propaganda and

agitation, which included setting up loudspeakers outside the office and having a car circulating in the community with loudspeakers on top. In between playing Malcolm X's records, someone would talk about the rally and its significance. By then we knew the members of the San Francisco Police Department's Tactical Squad stationed at the Northern Station, which covered the Fillmore District, and they knew us. Whenever we would see each other it would be a contest of insults.

One morning, Big Red, the most gung-ho of them, kept cruising by with a big grin on his face, shouting insults at whoever was on the loudspeaker outside our office. Then, in the beginning of the afternoon, he came by *driving* the car we had fitted with the loudspeakers! Obviously, Big Red had decided to have some fun. We were making phone calls to find out where the comrades in the car had been taken when someone from outside started shouting, "Here they come!" I looked out the door and saw Tactical Squad cars converging on the office from both directions. I told everyone to take cover, and they all ran upstairs. There were about fifteen people in the office at the time, about half being members of the community who were there getting information about the upcoming rally. Once I was sure everyone was out of sight, I went to the corner and took the twelve-gauge shotgun we had propped in the corner and started walking to the back of the office. At that instant, the front door was kicked in. With the shotgun in my hands, I knew if I made a move like I was going to turn around they would shoot me down, so instead I only turned my head just enough so I could see three of them, including Big Red, standing in the doorway with their M16s. Since I hadn't stopped walking, one of them said, "Stop and drop the gun." I only had a couple of steps to go before I would be at the doorway leading to the back of the office, so I kept walking and made a motion like I was going to lean the shotgun against the wall. Someone said, "Drop the gun or you're a dead man," but by that time I was close enough to the doorway that I was able to dive through it and behind the wall, where I was greeted by a big smile on the face of Eddie Griffin. The pigs at the door fell back, shouting, "They've got guns!" but I didn't share Eddie Griffin's smile because I knew we were at a great disadvantage. We had some guns, sure, but Panther offices at that time were not yet equipped to resist an attack. In fact, it was precisely that attack that subsequently prompted the order for all Panther offices to install the necessary equipment for defense against police assault.

With the pigs now gone, I crawled to the front of the office, with Griff Graff covering me, to check out the situation outside. I couldn't see a thing moving, and it was about that time they started lobbing the gas. And it wasn't ordinary tear gas. It was the stuff they were using in Vietnam that burned the skin, induced instant vomiting and mucus overproduction, and was both blinding and suffocating. Luckily, Griff and I were near the hole that had been cut in the wall as an alternate exit, and we called for everyone to come down and get out through the hole. Because they had all received the full effects of the gas by then, however, they were in pretty bad shape. Following the noise from our choking and gagging, the pigs ran around the block and trapped us all in the empty lot behind the office, telling everyone to spread their legs and lean against the wall with their hands up. My girlfriend Barbara was pretty sick and started slumping like she was going to pass out, and when I grabbed her to hold her up, Big Red shouted, "Nigger, I said put your hands up against the wall," and fired a burst from his M16. I don't know if he had intended to hit me or not, but after I was bailed out I went back to the site and stood by the bullet holes, which lined up at the height of my nose. Everyone was arrested, and almost everyone was released within an hour because there was really nothing anyone could be charged with. Cleve Brooks and I were the only ones held longer, and I don't know what Cleve was charged with, but I was charged with assault. After *they* had assaulted *our* office. That was exactly one of our definitions of pig: the aggressor posing as the victim. Big Red was quite an actor, and in court he gave an Academy Award–worthy performance telling the judge how I had dropped to one knee while pointing the shotgun at the officers. Anyone in their right mind would know that if I had made a move to turn around I would have been shot down.

A few weeks later, headquarters sent me to Boston and Detroit to iron out some organizational problems. The head of the Boston office, Charles "Chico" Neblett, didn't agree with the party line of making alliances with all progressive forces without regard to color, and he was refusing to pick up the Panther newspapers sent to the airport. In addition, he was showing signs of sudden wealth, which we found suspicious. He had bought a new Corvette Stingray and drove around in it wearing a big fur coat. It was clear to us that he must be ripping off funds from the party. He refused to go to headquarters and answer to that, so I expelled him and all his followers and reorganized the office under the leadership of Doug Miranda.

My traveling partner at this time was Robert "Spider" Webb. Spider had done two stretches in Vietnam, as a sergeant and "point man" on foot patrols, and had survived to tell about it. The point man on patrol is the easiest target and usually the first shot, so the fact that he was alive seemed proof that the Viet Cong hadn't wanted to kill him. Spider was wounded three times, but nothing serious. He used to visit Vietnamese families and, thanks to them, became politicized against the war. When he returned home, he came straight into the party.

Spider had migrated with his family from the South and lived up on Hunters Point. He always had a smile on his face and the calm that is characteristic of Southern rural blacks. Everyone loved Spider. When Huey was released from prison in August of 1970, Spider became one of his personal bodyguards, and it was no surprise since, because of his military training and experience, when you put a gun in Spider's hands it was like watching a ballet dancer. When he moved it was as if his body was made of a viscous fluid. He seemed to flow when he moved. He was a righteous Black Panther.

After things were more or less stabilized in Boston, we went on to Detroit, where it was only a matter of clarifying structure and rules, and getting the leadership to California. While there, I received an urgent phone call from headquarters telling me to go to New York and wait for David Hilliard, who was flying in.

I arrived in New York the night before the rendezvous, and while lying in bed listening to the news I learned that Alex Rackley, a Panther from the Harlem office, had been murdered in New Haven, Connecticut. The leadership of the party there had been arrested on charges of having killed nineteen-year-old Rackley because they suspected he was a police informant. Another blow.

As I entered the building for our meeting the next morning, two Panthers from the Bay Area that I knew very well were on their way out. They didn't stop, didn't smile, and only nodded their heads and kept stepping. I didn't know what was going on, but there was heavy tension in the air.

After the meeting with David was over, my next task was to find a place to stay for myself plus David and Robert Bay, who were not taking a flight back until the next morning. They were very uptight about having to spend the night; all the busts going on had them feeling insecure. I had a girlfriend in New

York who wasn't involved in any politics, so I took them to her pad to stay until it was time to go to the airport. Robert was so nervous he spent the night in a chair in the middle of the room with a .38 special in his hands. It's a good thing a cat didn't knock over a garbage can or something; given the state he was in, he might have shot us all.

Remembering when Bobby had told me that whenever I saw something that needed to be done to just do it, the next morning I informed David of my decision to stay on the East Coast to try to put the party there back together again after it had effectively been destroyed by the recent incidents in New Haven and New York. In New Haven the chapter literally didn't exist anymore, and in New York, after the bust of the Panther 21, everything was in limbo. All the people who had been sent from headquarters to organize the East Coast were either in jail or on the run, and it was obvious by David's and Robert's current attitudes that they were only concerned about getting out of town and saving their own skins. So, effectively, the East Coast had been abandoned. When I told him my plan, David looked at me like he thought I was crazy and said, "Deal with it." And with that, he and Robert split.

9

The Big Apple

NEW YORK, NEW YORK—the Big Apple. I thought it was a wild place, but it had a magnetic effect upon me. Coming from a place as quiet, clean, and relatively calm as San Francisco, my first impression was that it was the dirtiest place I had ever seen, with chuckholes in the streets big enough to stop a tank. I also noticed that in Harlem, at around five or six in the afternoon, the sidewalks filled up with people. The only time I had seen people in the streets like that in California, there was a riot or something. It turned out to be a traditional thing to do at that time of day, in part because few buildings had air conditioning and it would be suffocating inside in the summers.

The thing that disturbed me most was seeing the adults, kids, and even babies strung out on smack. Even the lampposts were leaning. It was sickening to see kids of nine or ten years old hanging onto a parking meter to keep from falling while they vomited their insides out. The most frightening of all was the fact that, after a few weeks, I began to get used to seeing such scenes. They were part of the landscape.

Working out of the Panther office on 7th Avenue, between 121st and 122nd Streets, I soon become aware that the representatives who had been sent from headquarters before me had alienated the few people that were still coming around after the 21 bust. They had arrived with the dogmatism and arrogance that most of us fall victim to when we have our first taste of Marxism-Leninism, embracing the tendency to think of ourselves as the sole possessors of truth. In the end, I would realize that true liberation will never come by that route.

The first thing I did in New York was attempt to neutralize any police agents still hanging around in the woodwork. I was authorized by headquarters to ban anyone from showing or even talking about weapons or military operations. Anyone violating that rule was automatically expelled. That way, if there were any agents still around trying to entrap anyone, they would have to show their hand. Later, one did.

There were several overt provocations carried out by different agencies while I was in New York. They had historically operated on fertile ground, since the city was so big that it wasn't possible for all the Panther members to know each other, as we did in the Bay Area. Our plan was that as long as everyone respected organizational discipline, the only way agents could get anything done was by breaking the rules and exposing themselves.

On one such occasion, FBI agents openly deposited money in the bank account of one of the heads of the Staten Island branch of the party. Some way or another the person in question was duped into accepting it, and the FBI doubtless had hopes that this would precipitate a reaction on our part of a magnitude that would permit them to come up with another conspiracy case. Being aware of that, however, we were able to devise a method of dealing with the situation without giving the bureau the opportunity to vamp on us. I looked for and found a doctor who agreed to administer a "truth serum" to the man who had accepted the FBI's money. When I offered the dupe the choice of expulsion from the party or an interrogation under the influence of the drug, he chose to resign. We knew we had him, and that was the end of the affair. Or so I thought.

Two days later the *Wall Street Journal*'s top front-page story was about the incident. In terms of everything else going on at that time, it didn't make sense why this story merited that level of attention—especially by the *Journal*, which is no scandal sheet—and to this day, I'm not really sure why they chose to run the story, but there's no doubt in my mind where they got their information. None of the other papers made mention of the affair.

There was another occasion when there was a clear case of entrapment. That time it turned out to be by the New York Police Department. One morning while listening to the news, Zayd Shakur and I were shocked to hear of the arrest of several Panthers in a roadblock at one of the exits of the West Side Highway. It was reported they were heavily armed and were on their way to carry out some military operation. The police said they had been tipped off and laid an ambush. They knew what car the Panthers would be in, its license number, and which exit they would be taking. By all the information they were giving out, it was obvious to us that the police had set up the operation themselves, through an embedded agent—an obvious attempt to strengthen the extremely weak case against the New York 21.

Zayd immediately called a press conference and condemned the arrests as an obvious police provocation, adding that if, by chance, there were any active Panthers lured into participating in the setup, they would be automatically expelled from the party. Everyone knew the standing rule that stipulated any member of the party that discussed, planned, or participated in any type of military operation was to be automatically expelled.

After we got the names of those involved, it was clear who

one of the agents was. He had previously tried, unsuccessfully, to infiltrate the Brooklyn branch of the party, but thanks to the new measures of security, he had been denied entry. Sure enough, just five hours after the highway incident took place, he was mysteriously bailed out. We got his home address from his application and took tape recorders and a camera there to interview him. We were surprised that he had given his correct address, but by the time we arrived, four black plainclothes policemen were already moving his belongings out of his apartment into a waiting van. We parked on the corner and watched the operation for a while, then split. It was obvious he was already in hiding and wouldn't be showing up.

The difficulty with that affair was the suffering of those who had allowed themselves to be entrapped. They had, openly and consciously, ignored party discipline, and yet after they were arrested they wanted the party to come to their rescue. It was difficult but necessary to enforce party rules and regulations. It was especially disturbing when the mother of one of the victims came to the office to ask aid for her son and I had to deny it. I felt that the security of the party had to take priority, and no exception could be made for those who openly violated discipline. The rules in question had been devised to protect members of the organization from just such provocations, and if we looked the other way on this first infraction, that would jeopardize everyone's security. It would have made us easy targets for all the other snakes lying in the cut, waiting to strike. There were already twenty-one people under indictment for conspiracy charges thanks to the work of at least five known agents who had not only infiltrated the party but had helped organize the New York branch at its inception. The only way I knew of to put an end to such activities was to enforce strict discipline.

Sharon and Zayd were my right and left hands. You couldn't find better comrades, and together we started slowly putting things back together. Contact with all progressive forces in the area was as solid as anyplace in the country, and I was calling headquarters practically every day asking for their help in fixing the party on the East Coast. One of the most urgent needs was for intensive political education. There really was no unity of ideas as to what the Panther party stood for anymore, and it wasn't doing any good having "Panthers" in the streets with everyone saying something different. Headquarters sent Sam Napier and sister Diane, a white woman from Los Angeles, who, as far as I knew, was not even in the party. She was a very close comrade, however, and had worked with the party in Los Angeles as well as visited and stayed with us in San Francisco.

One of the obstacles in working with the people on the East Coast was the fact that, since the 1920s, New York had been the citadel of black nationalism. For almost fifty years, the people in Harlem had been listening to leaders from Marcus Garvey to Elijah Muhammad and Malcolm X, and by the end of the 1960s, black nationalism was practically in their genes. Yet Hilliard had sent Diane, who was white, to help out. I could think of no one better to deal with the political education classes than her. She was into Marxism-Leninism long before any of us and was a perfect pedagogue. Luckily, we were able to convince everyone she was Mexican and turned a potential disaster into a good thing. Within a few weeks she had everyone more or less thinking along the same lines when they went out to do community work. This was all great for the party, but I couldn't help but think that Hilliard sending Diane was clear evidence of what he thought of my efforts to reorganize the East Coast.

After things had shaped up considerably, we organized a rally at a park in Harlem. I requested a speaker from headquarters, and David came. Despite pouring rain, the rally was a success, and David was apparently impressed with what he saw of our organizational efforts, because upon his return to headquarters he sent Al Carrol and JB to help out. That was all that was needed. Al and JB were from San Francisco, and you didn't have to tell them anything. They knew what to do.

One of the efforts we took seriously was the health and wellbeing of our members. After one of the Panthers started frequently falling sick and a doctor told us he was suffering from malnutrition, we immediately organized dinners in the offices every night for members, and everyone was to go work at one of the Free Breakfast for School Children Programs every morning, assuring each person had at least two meals a day. We also had volunteer doctors come to the office and give physical checkups to everyone. Organizationally, things were looking up.

Once the New York chapters were in good order, it became possible to start moving around the East Coast, with competent cadres moving in to help get things organized. The priority was dealing with the situation in New Haven. You couldn't get a Panther from headquarters to set foot there, and the former members who were now in jail had effectively been abandoned. To organize support for their defense, I chose people from different offices, then called Doug Miranda, and we went to New Haven. We held a rally in a park close to the downtown area and opened an office there the next day.

The authorities came close to getting me that time. The car I was driven around in turned out to be stolen, and they might have caught me if I hadn't ridden back from the rally in a different car. Doug left the rally in the hot car, however, and he was vamped on. When the pigs stopped him, the first thing out of their mouths was, "Where is DC?"—meaning me. Doug hadn't known the car was stolen either, and neither of us knew the police were on our tail. That explained why some of the agents attending the rally had been smiling and waving at me the whole time. After they busted Doug, I finally understood.

The next big mobilization was for the United Front Against Fascism Conference that the Panthers were organizing for July of 1969 in Oakland. The goal was to have progressive groups from the entire country represented at the conference. We made a swing through New Jersey, Pennsylvania, Maryland, and Washington, D.C., to drum up support for the conference. Barbara had already gone to Philadelphia, her hometown, to help the party there. When we passed through Baltimore we dropped off two comrades to help get things organized, and they were told we would be picking them up in about a week on the return trip. After things were finished in Washington we headed back through the places we'd been the week before, to check on progress.

Being in a hurry to get back to New York, I took the stairs at the Baltimore office two at a time. When I got to the door, however, someone stopped me and said don't come in. I asked what was going on and was told there was a pig in the closet—an agent they'd exposed within the party. I asked if he was dead; he said not yet. I asked how long had he been in there; he said three days. The temperature had been hitting one hundred every day, and I knew instantly that, finally, they had me. I knew that soon there would be another conspiracy case and that this time I would be included. Furious, I jumped back into the car and sped back to New York. I decided to do as much as I could before the fatal day came. That was in June of 1969.

Many of the conspiracy cases brought against the party were due to our own mistakes and excessive zeal whenever a police agent was discovered in our ranks. Instead of a small group dealing with things like that, whole branch offices got involved, and that always allowed the authorities to make sweeping arrests. We more or less delivered ourselves to the pigs with these conspiracy cases. I am convinced that most of their agents were sacrificed for the very purpose of allowing them to put whole chapters out of action. And that, of course, led to mistakes, like the case of Alex Rackley, the dead Panther at the center of the New Haven chapter's downfall.

Alex was an immigrant from the South and hadn't had any schooling. He couldn't read or write, and everyone knew that, but he loved the party and wanted to participate in everything, just like everyone else. That was still during the time of our *Little Red Book* worship. One day, someone went to the toilet and Alex was sitting there—he hadn't locked the door—and he had a *Red Book* in his hands. Open. I'm sure no one knows whether or not he even had it turned the right way, but what they saw had been enough to convince the New Haven leadership that Rackely was an agent, and for that he paid with his life. Stalin was not dead. It wasn't long before police swept through the organization and turned it inside out.

Despite the tension and suspicion we had to deal with, mobilization for the antifascism conference had gone well, and the event was a success, at least when it came to attendance. Movement representatives came from across the country—all very dedicated and conscious people—but politically, what a disaster. The Black Panther Party had more or less become the avant-garde of the entire radical movement, largely because of its combativeness and progressive political line, but that same dogmatism did not always combine well with the timidity of most white progressive organizations. Mainly due to a passive racism, whatever the Panthers said was law. And we all went for it, at least for a while.

Since I had been working on the East Coast, I didn't know exactly what was going to be on the program of the conference, but I knew it was our golden opportunity to get something going on a larger scale. There had never been such an assemblage of progressive forces in the contemporary history of the movement. When I arrived at headquarters for the conference and learned that the program was focused only on a plan for community control of the police, I couldn't believe my ears. They had to be kidding! But no, that was the program. After all the organizing and mobilizing of people to go all the way to Oakland, they were to be force-fed only that one small message. Nothing more. I was embarrassed—for everyone.

Why was I staying in the Panther party at that point? The main reason was because of my love and admiration for Huey and Eldridge, and the love I had for the party and what it had represented for me. I couldn't stop hoping that somehow things would get straightened out. One of the most powerful forces that kept me in the party was the deep comradeship that I had come to know for the first time in my life. I had developed relationships so deep and confident that I was willing to put my life in the hands of certain comrades. At that time, I wasn't capable of thinking about being separated from them.

After the conference, I returned to New York and plunged into dealing with community problems, hoping to eliminate the negative thoughts that were becoming more and more inexorable. I was beginning to realize there was no one among us capable of coming up with a correct strategy, neither short- nor long-term, for leading the struggle. I had no illusions about my own capabilities and knew I didn't have any ideas either. So I drowned my anguish in community work.

It had been recently announced that the clothing allowance for welfare children was to be suppressed at the beginning of the school year, and so we decided to show our solidarity with those who would be deprived. We canvassed the entire city for donations of clothing and shoes, and we would pass everything out the week before school was to open. The Free Clothing Program was launched.

We also came face-to-face with other groups organizing the black community in the area. On 125th Street and 7th Avenue a group protesting the destruction of buildings to make room for an office tower paid for by a Rockefeller had occupied the lot and brought the work to a standstill. The people involved in the occupation were philosophically part of the black nationalism movement, which was strongly against the Panther position of working with all progressive forces regardless of race, but in the spirit of progress, two nights a week we went with the entire Harlem branch of the Panthers to the lot to wage fierce ideological battles with this group, an exercise that ended up being productive for everyone. After a few sessions, it became clear that those running the hardest line had embraced capitalism, and most of them had a particular interest in or were owners of "black shops." It was always amazing to hear them arguing against working with whites and then turning the discussion to the need for blacks to stick together and come to their shops and buy one of their fifty-dollar dashikis.

In contrast, Fred Hampton, the young leader of the Chicago branch of the party, had organized the Rainbow Coalition with white immigrants from Appalachia, who had formed their own organization, called the Patriot Party, which had been modeled after the Panthers. Like blacks, they were cooped up in ghettos and suffered many of the same problems, and the goal of the Rainbow Coalition was to join forces to mobilize these and other struggling communities. Inspired by this group, we decided to make a daring move to help in our efforts to break the hold of the hardline black nationalists in New York. We started organizing a rally at P.S. 201 in Harlem and invited William "Preacherman" Fesperman, chairman of the Patriot Party, to speak.

At this same time, we were also working with the Young Lords, a Puerto Rican organization modeled after the Panthers, who had come from Chicago to ask for our help in organizing a chapter of the Lords in Spanish Harlem. Our coalition was so strong that we worked hand in hand on all activities, but when Felipe Luciano, the chairman of the New York branch, heard we were bringing in Preacherman, he got uptight. He said it would be a disaster to bring in a white to speak at a Harlem rally.

The day of the rally, we still didn't know whether Felipe would speak as representative of the Lords. In the end, he did turn up, but in an effort to distance his Young Lords group from the Panthers' endorsement of Preacherman's Young Patriots, he showed up to speak wearing a dashiki. Although Felipe had predicted all kinds of problems, and possibly even attacks from nationalist groups, the rally was a success, and after Preacherman spoke and made it clear that our problems were the same, regardless of color, he received a standing ovation. I basked in the glow of seeing niggers of Harlem, dressed in African clothes, standing and cheering Preacherman, who was white. The rally was a smash, and as far as I know it was the first of its kind in the contemporary history of the struggle in Harlem. Such experiences reinforced my optimism and my belief that if people are given the correct information about their situations, the usual problems (like racism) can be checked enough to allow them to work together to bring about changes that would be beneficial to everyone.

These small successes kept me going, even in the face of other trials. As the representative of the central committee on the East Coast, I had to deal with many meetings and speaking engagements, and it seemed that, without exception, everywhere I went I was challenged, and in a more or less hostile manner, to clarify the Panthers' position on the Middle East. I initially had to decline comment given my ignorance of the region's complicated history, but the persistence of such questions obliged me to read as many books as possible about the history of Zionism and the state of Israel. What a Pandora's box that turned out to be.

After intensive research I learned that Israel was created by a vote at the United Nations that had been undertaken without consulting the people—namely the Palestinians—who already lived in the territory; it was, as I understood it, essentially a way of easing the guilt of the Europeans in the wake of the Holocaust, and also a way of eliminating their "Jewish problem." It seemed to me that the ideas of Theodor Herzl, the father of Zionism, and Elijah Muhammad, the founder of the Black Muslims, were about the same things, and also that their efforts were born of similar desperation—desperation to the point that they could see no other solution to their problems than to acquire territory where their people could live separate from everyone else. Just as the Panthers had derided black nationalism as "pork-chop nationalism," I began calling Zionism "kosher nationalism." The economic base of the support for the creation of the state of Israel was to be found in its strategic location. I wrote an article in the summer of 1969 for the Panther paper stating so, and nothing that has occurred in the years since has compelled me to change my mind.

In the article, I talked of Menachem Begin, who headed the Irgun, a terrorist group that had massacred the inhabitants of a village called Deir Yassin in April 1948. The attackers then circulated around the territory with loudspeakers on their vehicles warning other Palestinians to remember Deir Yassin. They were told that if they didn't want the same thing to happen to them they should flee their homes and leave the territory. It is sad to note that even today Palestinian people are still having their land taken from them and seeing their centuries-old homes bulldozed into dust.

History can be a trap. It all depends where you slice it. If we look at it from the biblical time when the Jewish diaspora was created, we must recognize that all the nomadic tribes that lived in the area did not leave, and many of their descendants had been there through 1948 and beyond. I cannot justify putting the rights of the Jewish descendants who left above the rights of the Palestinian descendants who stayed. The fact that different tribes adopted different religions is irrelevant. Also, the fact of supporting the struggle of the Palestinian people can in no way be called anti-Semitism. That is only a historical distortion used by Zionists to intimidate people and garner sympathy. Because in reality both Palestinians and Jews are Semitic peoples. It is a fratricidal struggle. The Palestinian people are the descendants of those who stayed, and the Jews are the descendants of those who left in the diaspora. That is historical fact. If there ever were to be a moral Judgment Day, I wouldn't want to be counted among the sympathizers of Zionism.

I caught hell in New York when I started running that line. At one time the Jewish Defense League made the mistake of sending a group of their militants to set up a picket line outside the Harlem Panther office, and while we went inside and locked the door, the people of the community showed them no mercy and kicked their asses and ran them out of town. Xenophobia is a universal phenomenon.

The family of Joseph A. Cox, Don Cox's grandfather, Appleton, Missouri, 1901; *from left to right*: Bernice, Joseph A. Cox, Mabel, Fred, Josephine, Alice Müller Cox, and Harry in center. (*Family collection*)

Sister Marleeta (age seven), unidentified family friend, Don Cox (age six), Sedalia, Missouri, 1943. (*Family collection*)

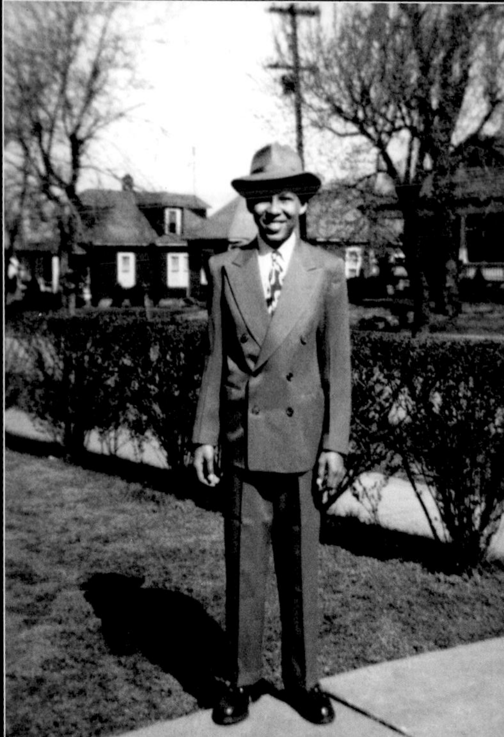

Don Cox (age thirteen) on the way to Taylor Chapel Methodist Church, Sedalia, Missouri, 1949. (*Family collection*)

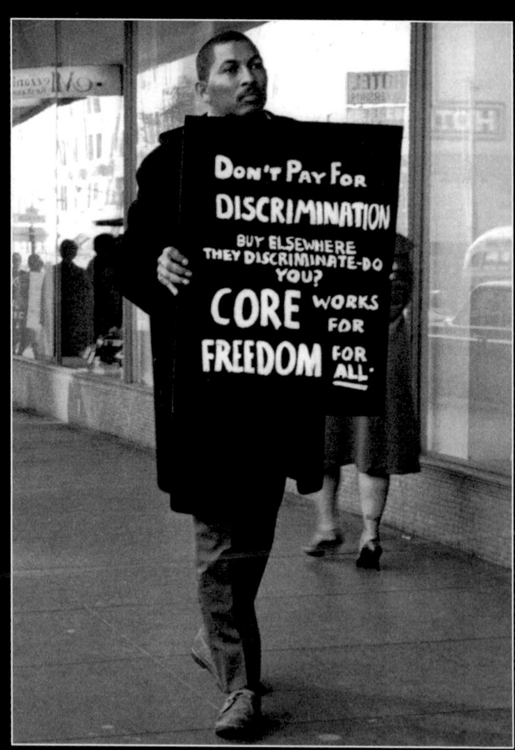

Picketing to end discrimination at Macy's, San Francisco, December 1963. (*Family collection*)

Relaxing at sister Irene's house in Milpitas, California, 1967. (*Family collection*)

On road trip to Missouri to visit family; *from left to right*: Iris Cox, Don Cox, son Donnie (age four), and daughter Kimberly (age ten), 1967.
(*Family collection*)

Don Cox speaking at the United Front Against Fascism Conference, Oakland Auditorium, July 19, 1969, Oakland, California. (*Copyright 2018 by Stephen Shames/Polaris; used by permission*)

Don Cox at Vietnam Moratorium rally, Polo Fields at Golden Gate Park, San Francisco, November 15, 1969. (*Copyright 2018 by Stephen Shames/Polaris; used by permission*)

Don Cox speaking at a Free Huey Newton/Free Bobby Seale rally, Federal Building, San Francisco, February 1970. (*Copyright 2018 by Stephen Shames/Polaris; used by permission*)

Don Cox with Felicia and Leonard Bernstein at their Park Avenue apartment for cocktail party to raise money to defend the Panther 21, New York City, January 14, 1970. (*Copyright 2018 by Stephen Salmieri; used by permission*)

Standing in front of Black Panther Party National Headquarters, Berkeley, February 1970; *from left to right*: June Hilliard, Don Cox, Elbert "Big Man" Howard; staged for *Newsweek* cover, issue of February 23, 1970. (*Copyright 2018 by Stephen Shames and the Estate of Alan Copeland; used by permission*)

Don Cox, seated with sandals, with unidentified Panthers and Algerian officials, and Eldridge Cleaver in foreground, press conference in Villa Boumaraf, Algiers, September 11, 1970. (*Photograph by Dominique Berretty, The Black Star Collection/Ryerson Image Centre; used by permission*)

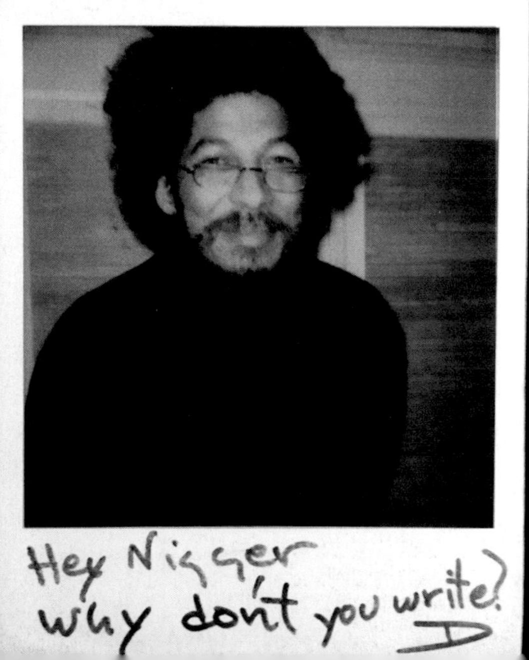
Hey Nigger
why don't you write?
D

Polaroid of Don Cox encouraging his son, Donnie, to write, Paris, France, circa 1980. (*Family collection*)

Don Cox in Ghana, circa 1982. (*Family collection*)

Outside home in Camps-sur-l'Agly, France, 2009. (*Family collection*)

10

Radical Chic

THE DAY OF THE RALLY to give away the clothing donations arrived. People lined up two deep, around the block, in both directions. The next day I flew to headquarters, and the plane was held up by two FBI agents who came on board to congratulate me for the success of our efforts. Then they left and the plane took off. Those were some weird types at the FBI. I wonder if they really thought I cared what they thought.

On one occasion, two of them kept circling the block where our office was located. When they saw me on one pass, they motioned that I come to their car. I shook my head no and motioned for them to come to me, and I sat on the bench in front of the office. They came. They told me, with the straightest faces, that they were representatives of President Nixon and that the president wanted to know just what it was that we wanted. With that, I went into my act. I started by running down the Panther party's ten-point platform and program. I then demanded the immediate release of our chairman, Bobby Seale, and the rest of the people in New Haven, plus Huey, the New York 21, and every other political prisoner I could think of. They stood calmly the whole time, and when I finished they thanked me and left. Weird people.

Several months after the Panthers in New Haven had been arrested, Bobby had been busted and included in the conspiracy case. He was an innocent victim, like I was in Baltimore; we both just happened to pass through the respective cities while some shit was going on that we had nothing to do with. But the authorities seized any opportunity they had to further weaken the party.

By then Eldridge had surfaced in Algiers. Having jumped bail in the Bay Area after being arrested for the shootout with the Oakland police, he'd gone to Cuba, where he'd stayed for six months. Others had also gone there to escape the mounting repression in America, including Byron Booth and Rahim Smith (a.k.a. Clinton Robert Smith, Jr.), who in January of 1969 had escaped together from prison in California and hijacked a plane the next day to Cuba to join Eldridge. Akili (a.k.a. James Patterson) and his wife, Gwen, from the Brooklyn branch had gone there also. The Cuban experience had been far from satisfactory, and ultimately they would leave to join Eldridge in Algiers, which, with Cuba, was at that time governed by revolutionaries and was therefore sympathetic to other struggling revolutionaries. In July of that year, the central committee went to Algiers to visit Eldridge and to participate in the Pan-African Cultural Festival, a gathering of nations and representatives of liberation movements. Unfortunately, my work in New York did not permit me to go that time, but I intended to make the trip at my first opportunity.

Even though I had been flying out to the West Coast headquarters every two weeks, I had been out of touch on the day-to-day happenings of the party since the antifascism conference. I did, however, begin seeing deterioration in the relationships between people in the party. I was noticing an atmosphere of tension and fear building among former comrades, and one thing was clear: Hilliard was ruling with an iron hand. With Bobby in jail in New Haven, that left Hilliard alone in charge. One of the things I was shocked to learn was that party members were being disciplined for misbehavior by being kept in a makeshift jail under headquarters. At one point, there had been a team digging an emergency escape tunnel under headquarters, but after they had hit water and had to abandon the project, the hole was turned into a jail cell where Panthers who displeased the leadership could be thrown. David's brother, June, was the jailer. He carried a blackjack in his pocket and people feared he wouldn't hesitate to hit someone in the head with it for the slightest disagreement.

When we started studying Marxism-Leninism, David had always been one of the strongest at manipulating words and ideas for his purposes, but the very strongest was Masai (Raymond) Hewitt, who had been a member of a Marxist group in Los Angeles before joining the Panthers. He was well schooled in dialectical materialism, and that's why he was made minister of education. It was Masai who conducted the party's first political education classes. Now, however, in order for David to consolidate his control of the party, it was imperative that he crush Masai. Masai, being one of the leaders not then in jail, was the only thing between David and undisputed leadership. As I traveled between New York and the San Francisco Bay Area, I noticed something was happening to Masai, although at first I couldn't recognize what it was. It was only when I flew in one weekend and discovered that Masai had been hit in the head with the blackjack and put in the hole that I began to understand. He was being punished for something ridiculously insignificant, and it was clear to me then that he was being "tamed." After that, every time I saw Masai, he was silent. He seemed to talk only when he was asked something directly—Masai, the one who had first helped us understand *On Practice* by Mao.

When I finally understood what was going on, I became

even more cautious; only "yes people" were kept at headquarters at that time, and I knew that if I ever said or did anything that upset David, he could do with me what he wanted. I vowed then that if I managed to not be killed by the Panthers, I would live to see them regret they hadn't found a way to do it. The only hope I saw for the party then was that Charles Garry was still working to get Huey out of prison. Huey was our only hope. But Garry had better hurry or there wouldn't be anything left of the party to straighten out. Denunciations had become a regular thing, and expulsions were the order of the day—and no longer just for legitimate causes and to clean up the party, but now to get rid of people David or June didn't like. After people were expelled, there would be an article in the Panther paper denouncing them for being agents provocateurs, pigs, crazy, or something else. The Panther paper became a tool of defamation.

It got to the point that the mass line became the party line. In other words, if someone said anything about, for example, one of the conspiracy cases and their position didn't coincide exactly with the propaganda that was being put out by headquarters, they were branded a traitor. After severe physical punishment they would then be expelled and denounced in the paper.

Take the case in Baltimore, for example. The pig they had in the closet turned out to be a real police agent who had infiltrated the branch, and when that was discovered, he was killed. I wasn't there, and I don't know any details, nor am I prepared to pass judgment as to whether that particular agent should have been killed or not, but I can say that doing things that way worked against the goal of developing the consciousness of people, which was what we were supposed to be focused on. People can learn from negative experiences as well as positive ones, perhaps even more so.

On one of my trips to headquarters, David told me to go to Algiers and see Eldridge. I was pleasantly surprised. There was nothing I wanted to do more than that. I got my passport and made reservations for about three weeks later. Emory Douglas and Judy Hart (now Judy Juanita) also would be going. It was the first good excitement I had felt for some time.

The next week, back in New York, I was heading to my pad after a day's work at the Harlem office when I spotted cars full of men parked all over the neighborhood. There was no doubt in my mind that they finally had my number. I rushed into the pad and told my girlfriend Susanne that pigs were all over the place and to start making phone calls. And then I immediately went outside. I didn't want them to bust into the pad; there was too much valuable equipment that would be lost. Some of them were already walking up the other side of the street, and when they saw me come back out, they froze. If I had any hopes they were in the neighborhood to deal with something else, those hopes were laid to rest. My plan then was to try to get into the subway, but when I looked over my shoulder, they were piling out of cars on both sides of the street and some were already walking fast in my direction. I ran into the bar on the corner, but the bartender couldn't make change I needed for the phone, so I ran back outside, where at least I could attract a crowd.

As I stepped outside, I was surrounded and arrested. I asked for what and was relieved to hear them start talking about violation of some gun laws. I didn't really understand what it was all about, but since I hadn't heard the word Baltimore, I had new confidence and went into my act. I demanded to see a warrant, which they didn't have, as it hadn't yet arrived from San Francisco, and then I started hollering for help, saying that I was being kidnapped, et cetera. I could have won an Oscar for my performance that night.

It turns out they were agents from the alcohol, tobacco, and tax bureau of the Treasury Department. They were responsible for enforcing the federal gun laws that had just been passed, and the federal district attorney of Northern California had decided to arrest me as a test case for a new law that stipulated it was a felony offense for an ex-felon to have a firearm in his possession. (The felony was from when I was busted working for the post office more than a decade before.) The gun in question was the one I had supposedly used to assault the police who had attacked our office in San Francisco back in April. It was now November. They were going to take the case all the way to the Supreme Court, meaning that I was likely going to be convicted, with each appeal we might make being denied all the way up to the Supreme Court. It was a way for the feds to keep me hung up in courts.

When they took me to their offices, it was clear they weren't regular police types. There was some young rookie standing in the hallway jumping up and down saying, "Good work, good work." Real square. It was his boss—the head of the office—who had led the raid. When they went to fingerprint me, it had been so long since they had busted anyone, the ink pad had dried up.

I asked to be allowed to make the phone call I was entitled to and then dialed direct to the Panther office in Berkeley. David came to the phone, went into a rage, and started cursing and threatening me. I was speechless. He thought I had arranged to get myself busted to avoid going to Algiers to see Eldridge. I couldn't understand why he would think I would want to *avoid* seeing Eldridge.

I was taken to the federal holding jail, and not only was I fingerprinted there but I was body-printed too. I had never heard of such a thing. I still wonder if that was normal. They had me rolling in ink—arms, legs, chest, and back. It might have been done to intimidate me, and the most uncomfortable thing was being sent to my cell naked.

I was taken to court the next day. The federal prosecutor asked that my passport be confiscated, and although the judge denied his request, he did uphold the request that I be restricted to New York, my place of residence, and to San Francisco, the location of the court where I was to answer to the charges against me. At last, the police had the means to keep me from traveling around doing my job. I was convinced that had my passport been confiscated, Hilliard would have sworn it was a setup on my part to avoid making the trip to Algiers. Murray Kempton, a New York writer and journalist, bailed me out of jail. (He would later write a book on the New York 21 called *The Briar Patch: The People of the State of New York versus Lumumba Shakur, et al.*, for which he received the National Book Award in 1974.) Given Hilliard's reaction on the phone, I'm not sure he would have allowed the party to bail me out.

Upon my release I flew to headquarters. When I saw Hilliard, he started ranting and raving like a madman, saying things like, "You better get your ass over to Algiers. I don't care what they said about you traveling." I no longer understood anything or what I was supposed to do. Later, I overheard him talking in the next room to Connie Matthews, the party's international coordinator, saying, "Well, if he's not a pig then he's got nothing to worry about." I began to see a pattern. Masai had been neutralized and now it was my turn, even though if *anyone* knew of my honesty and devotion to the struggle, it was David. There was no way he could believe I was an agent, not with all he knew about me. Yet it was clear that he was going to neutralize me by trying to convince others I was a pig. I relaxed a little then, knowing he would never succeed with that. Nevertheless, I made a point of avoiding him until I went to Algiers.

Finally, the big day arrived. I was going to see Eldridge again. When Judy, Emory, and I arrived at Orly airport in Paris, Ellen Wright, the widow of author Richard Wright, and Julia Herve, their daughter, met us at the airport. They invited us to the airport restaurant while we waited for the flight to Algiers. To reach the restaurant, we had to pass through customs into French territory, and as soon as we did, some men in civilian clothes flashed us official-looking identification cards and asked us to follow them. Apparently, they were from some branch of French intelligence, but it seemed clear they were working at the behest of the Americans. They took us into a back room and literally tore our luggage apart. A uniformed policeman did the searching and seemed to really like his job. He threw stuff everywhere. He was as nasty as any pig I had seen in the States. We were finally let go, but not in time to catch the flight to Algiers. Ellen then invited us to spend the night at her house.

We called Eldridge and headquarters and got the order to immediately set up a picket line in front of the New York offices of Air France and their United Nations mission. The French authorities had to be shown they couldn't mess with us with impunity. When we returned to the airport to take the next scheduled flight to Algiers, we were again taken to the back room, and again we were released after the flight had left. We were furious to see the French authorities kissing ass and doing the Americans' dirty work. We went back to Ellen's, made more phone calls, and requested that influential friends of the Panthers intervene at the French embassy in Washington and lodge a protest against our treatment at Orly. Something apparently worked along the line, and when we returned the next day for the last flight to Algiers, we passed through without incident.

On the way to the gate, I heard a voice calling, "Monsieur Cox, Monsieur Cox," and I turned to see a policeman running down the hall carrying one of my file folders. Not only had we been harassed by the authorities, but it turned out they were thieves as well. I wondered how the folder had been stolen right in front of my eyes; when they were going through our stuff in the back room, I thought I was watching their every move. The file that had been taken contained letters from families of prisoners held in Vietnam. It was well known that the Panthers had relations with the Vietnamese people, and headquarters had received many letters from Americans whose family members were prisoners of war in Vietnam. They thought we might be able to forward the messages to their captive loved ones. Obviously, that upset the powers that be, who took it as a blow that people who had sons, brothers, cousins, fathers, and uncles imprisoned in Vietnam felt more confident going through the Panther party than the government. That was why we had been targeted; Washington got their French lackeys to do their bidding. Even stranger, the policeman who returned my file asked if I would give him the stamps on the envelopes to keep as a souvenir.

Finally we arrived in Algiers. I was impressed by our reception at the airport in Dar El Beïda. I was also amused to discover that Dar El Beïda means "white house." Security men at the airport took us out of line and expedited all the formalities, and then we found Eldridge, Rahim, and Byron, who were waiting for us. As we drove through Algiers on our way to Eldridge's pad out in Pointe Pescade, I had images of Pontecorvo's film *Battle of Algiers* swimming in my head. Pointe Pescade was where Ali la Pointe, the movie's main character, was from—that's where the "Pointe" came from in his name—and I was thrilled to be in revolutionary territory.

After greeting Kathleen, we sat down to talk. Eldridge wanted to know what was going on back at headquarters. Not knowing exactly what he knew, I kept quiet, waiting for a clue, hoping to see exactly where he was coming from. He told me David had sent me to Algiers for them to kill me! I felt like I'd been hit by a sledgehammer.

My head started reeling. I couldn't think. I didn't really hear anything else that Eldridge said, although after a couple of tokes of good North African hash, I calmed down a bit—enough to understand that, as far as Eldridge was concerned, the Black Panther Party was conducting itself like a bunch of sissies. He pulled out Panther newspapers from the past few months to show me that there were no longer any images of guns in the paper. He couldn't see where the party was going. I was speechless. Those past months I had spent my energies getting support organized for the New York 21 and the people in New Haven, in addition to doing community work, and being so isolated from the center of power and decision-making that I hadn't noticed the changes in the paper. I was well aware, of course, that it had become a tool Hilliard used to condemn those in his disfavor, but the political shift had slipped right past me. Eldridge, however, saw it for what it was: the party was floundering. I agreed but had no ideas about what should be done.

When Byron asked why Hilliard wanted to get rid of me, I really didn't know. Having nothing but the desire to see the Panther party become the force capable of leading the struggle, I couldn't see why anyone would want to reproach me. I was sure my devotion to the struggle and the party was as strong as anyone else's, if not stronger. I couldn't think of anything I had done to get on David's bad side. Perhaps Hilliard wanted me out of the way because San Francisco had some of the most devoted and disciplined people as could be found anywhere in the party—people devoted to the struggle and not to any personal gain—and maybe Hilliard felt threatened by that. At the time, I gave no thought to his thirst for absolute power. As someone who never had any thoughts about personal power, and being mostly unaware about the effects of such power on some leaders' mentalities, I had overlooked that aspect of things.

As was the case for Stalin, Hilliard did not have among many Panthers the moral authority that came of being respected within the party for his integrity, courage, or devotion to the struggle. The only thing that had put him in the position of power as the highest-ranking member of the party was the circumstance of the struggle—specifically that he was the only remaining leader not in jail or exile at the time. There was a vacuum of leadership at the top and so, within the party, he had taken it upon himself to exercise power and authority using force and repression. Thinking back, it's too bad he didn't show some of that same viciousness the night Li'l Bobby was killed. Hilliard was one of those arrested in the shootout, and he was found hiding under a bed in the house next door—the house some policemen had stood on to shoot down at Li'l Bobby and Eldridge.

Feeling relieved to know Eldridge was not against me, the rest of my stay in Algiers was exciting, especially because I got to meet representatives of liberation movements from all over the world. It was the first time I was able to see the effects of our movement on the international level. Blacks in America were seen by many foreigners as being at the forefront of the worldwide struggle of oppressed people seeking liberation. Our courage was considered exemplary because we were actually struggling from inside the boundaries of the dominant world power.

My devotion to the struggle was only deepened by all those new contacts. I met Elaine Klein (later known as Elaine Mokhtefi), who worked at the ministry of information, having left the States in 1951, during the McCarthy period, for France, where she stayed for ten years. She had gone back to work at the United Nations with the Algerian Office—as the unofficial Algerian mission at the UN was known during the war of liberation from the French—and after independence, she moved to Algeria in 1962. Soon she was working in President Ahmed Ben Bella's press and information office, and she continued to live in Algeria even after the coup that brought Houari Boumédiène to power in 1965. More than any person, she was responsible for arranging the Panthers' welcome in Algiers, and Eldridge's especially. She is the one who made all the necessary contacts, and I hope she will always be remembered for that. Through Elaine, we also met Zorah Sellami, who worked with Elaine and later became the wife of Ben Bella.

We were invited to the embassy of the National Liberation Front of Vietnam to celebrate their national day. That was a great honor for us. Little did we know that, later, their villa in the El Biar sector of the city was to become our embassy, where we would house the International Section of the Black Panther Party.

One day during my Algiers trip, I received an urgent phone call from R. J. Engel, my lawyer. He told me that the judge assigned to my case was giving me forty-eight hours to report to him or he would issue a warrant for my arrest. I'm sure the judge did that at the request of the CIA or the FBI; if they hadn't been involved, the judge would have just waited until my next scheduled court appearance.

I had little choice but to curtail my Algiers visit and return to San Francisco. On my way back through the Orly airport

nothing about it. I wanted to always have the psychological edge when dealing with David.

Unfortunately, he refused to let me return to New York, saying I was messing up back there. I knew that was only an excuse to put one of his own flunkies in my place, and the man he picked was Robert Bay. Once I'd gotten things organized and running fairly smooth—including garnering support for the New York 21 and the people in New Haven—Hilliard was ready to go back in and take control. He could lie and say whatever he wanted about me, but the organization of the Panther party on the East Coast in December of 1969 compared to what it was in the spring of that year was irrefutable proof I hadn't fucked up all that bad.

This was the time when I finally made the decision to leave the party. Now I just had to figure out how I could do it without having my name smeared in the Panther paper, or being killed. In the meantime I just hung around headquarters in the East Bay or at the San Francisco office. The federal authorities had effectively clipped my wings, and since Hilliard said I couldn't go to New York, I was stuck in the Bay Area. I moved to Hunters Point, which had always been a magnet for me. I was comfortable there.

I also got busy in the community, helping where I could. Synanon, a local drug-rehab organization, made contact and said that if I would participate in their weekly "criticism" sessions, they would give the party some of the tons of surplus food stored in their warehouse. That was a real bonanza; I would have gone twice a week if they had asked. After the Free Breakfast for School Children Program, the free health clinics, and the Free Clothing Program, we now had a Free Food Program!

Synanon was helpful to us, but it was also rather strange.

In terms of helping people withdraw from heroin, Synanon had great success, but the weakness I saw in their system at that time was that most of the ex-addicts could not function in the outside world. As long as they lived inside the Synanon environment, they were okay, but once they left, there were many re-shoots. The artificial environment inside Synanon became just as indispensable to them as heroin once had been. I also found the format of their "criticism" or "character destruction" sessions problematic. After my experiences with people off the streets, including junkies, I had become a firm believer in criticism and self-criticism, but only if it was used constructively. Synanon's approach was to have its members endure aggressive criticism from fellow members during special therapy sessions, and I could never get behind the idea that personal attacks to try to hurt someone was an effective way of getting them to improve their lives. I believed in comrades helping each other and forging unity; in my experience, that seemed to work as an incentive toward positive action. Anyway, we got the food from Synanon and the people in the community were happy, so it all worked out. On Hunters Point, every family on the hill got at least one bag, and there was always enough food to distribute on both sides of the bay. Needless to say, that solidified the Panthers' ties with the community, not to mention our security; after the first day's distribution, the neighbors around the office would report to us every time they saw a police car pass by.

When Emory and Judy finally returned from Algiers, Charles Garry, the Panthers' attorney, called a meeting with Emory, David, and myself. The tone and nature of his questioning was my first indication that all was not well between the "leadership" of the party and Eldridge. When we were asked our evaluation of Eldridge's behavior, Emory kept repeating,

"The man's crazy, the man's crazy," but he gave no details to substantiate what he was saying. After all I had seen from the current leadership, I assumed we were basically being asked to discredit Eldridge. And I wasn't going for it. I decided that at the first opportunity I was going to join Eldridge in Algiers. To hell with all this shit. As far as I was concerned, the party was finished, and it was just a matter of time before that would be clear for all to see.

With the repression that had come down on the party from the authorities—not unexpected given our philosophy—those making the decisions started backing away from each other and kept on backing away until the final split. I was not aware of any attempt to devise new strategies and tactics to deal with the present conditions, and it seemed that the days of action were long behind us, leaving nothing but a lot of empty rhetoric and profanity. The Panther party had become quite expert at identifying the problems and the real enemies, but in terms of analysis toward developing strategies, giving directions, and providing leadership to the struggle, zero. Nothing! Other than the few community programs, the only activity the Panthers were engaged in was defense work for all the comrades behind bars.

I guess to keep me cool, Hilliard told me I could go to New York for a few days if I wanted. I caught the first thing smoking. I arrived at the moment our defense committee, headed by a white radical named Marty Kenner, had organized a fundraising affair for the New York 21 at the Manhattan pad of Broadway composer and conductor Leonard Bernstein and his wife, Felicia. The Bernsteins, along with friends of theirs, were alarmed at the growing repression against the Panthers and wanted to hear, straight from the horse's mouth, just what we were all about. I went to their Park Avenue penthouse that night to represent the central committee.

It was a curious evening to say the least. Felicia Bernstein seemed to be a genuinely concerned person, and Leonard was also, but he was a good actor, so I don't know if he really showed himself that night. Otto Preminger, the film director, appeared to be the most politically conscious of anyone there, and broadcast journalist Barbara Walters was the most honest. She made it clear that she would never allow me in her house and that she didn't approve of our activities; she only wanted to know if, in order for us to have what we wanted, she would have to give up her own comforts. Harry Belafonte's wife, Julie Robinson, was the most relaxed, and opera singer Leontyne Price the most cowardly. While she and I were standing talking, someone approached us with a camera and she fled.

That night we managed to collect a decent sum to help toward bail money for the New York 21, but it was writer Tom Wolfe who profited most from the evening. He wrote a lengthy article about the affair for *New York* magazine and then later the same year turned it into a book, *Radical Chic & Mau-Mauing the Flak Catchers*, which received a wide readership. I wonder how much he made off all that. I never liked leeches and sneaks. He had snuck in with a small tape recorder and recorded the whole evening so he could profit from the repression of the Panthers and mock our efforts to raise funds to free people who were subsequently found to be innocent, which we knew was the case all along. One who profits from the misery of others is a leech of the worst kind. Years later I heard him give his version of things on a French cultural radio station; he said his work got us good publicity, but that doesn't hold water for me. The Panthers were in no need of publicity help in those days, not with all the media coverage we were getting on our own. A full-page article about the party ran in the society section of the *New York Times* the next day, written by columnist Charlotte Curtis, who had been in attendance.

As this layer of American society began to give us support, the reaction from the authorities was immediate and fierce. They launched a national campaign of slander and intimidation against what they, following Tom Wolfe, called "radical chic." Many of our supporters from that class were intimidated and retreated, and the rest of the evenings we had planned similar to the Bernstein affair were canceled. I had a secret meeting with Felicia Bernstein at the studio where she painted, and she told me of the misery she and Leonard had endured since the night of the gathering. They had been receiving constant hate mail and phone calls, including threats to their lives. She wanted to know if there was anything I could do to help. I could think of nothing, other than to reiterate my belief that all people should stand up and defend what they believe. Otherwise, fascism has fertile ground in which to grow.

As a result of all the noise about the Bernstein gathering, talk show host Dick Cavett asked that I appear on his show. The opportunity to get our views across to a nationwide audience could not be passed up, and although I was uptight about it, having never overcome my timidity when speaking before groups, I was obliged to accept this type of public engagement because there were so few of us left in the Panther leadership. It was an uneventful evening, and it was disappointing but not unexpected that the show followed the typical practice of inviting a "Tom" to balance out the presence of a militant. I remembered the same tactic being used whenever Malcolm X went on TV or radio—using blacks to trap other blacks in contradictions. In this case, I was put up against Eleanor Holmes Norton, a black lawyer who worked for the American Civil Liberties Union. She had successfully defended a free speech case for Alabama's segregationist governor George Wallace. It seems that Wallace's civil rights had been violated, and when he called upon the

ACLU to defend him, they successfully did so, using a black lawyer. How sinister can you get? Not wanting to be tricked into a conflict on live TV, coast to coast, with another black person, which was exactly what they wanted, I only said I thought it was possible for a person to be too objective, using the black lawyer as an example. Walking in Harlem the next day, I was stopped by some Black Muslims selling newspapers who congratulated me on how I dealt with the situation.

Jean Genet, the French novelist and writer of the play *The Blacks*, was in liaison with the Panther support group in France, headed by Michel Persitz, and he decided to come to America to help us organize support for political prisoners in the intellectual community. He was denied entry, but thanks to the efforts of Persitz and Connie Matthews, Genet was eventually let in and he made his way to our Bay Area headquarters.

Genet couldn't believe his eyes when he saw how we were living. The armor plates and sandbags guarding all windows and doors, with portholes for shooting out of, was something he couldn't reconcile with his image of the United States of America, the land of the free and the home of the brave. With the constant attacks on Panther offices across the country, however, he quickly understood over the course of his visit the necessity of such measures. While in the States, he moved from coast to coast, waging struggle on behalf of political prisoners. He was tireless. He had arrived with only the clothes on his back, his sole "luggage" his wallet containing what appeared to be hundreds of scraps of paper with scribbling on them, all of them held together with rubber bands and stuffed into his back pocket.

While he was in Berkeley, we had been invited to an afternoon cocktail party organized at writer Jessica Mitford's home on Regent Street. Jean, Masai, Emory, David, and I went to talk about the repression being waged against the party. Tom Hayden and Stew Albert, two of our staunchest allies from the radical white movement, were also present. The rest were mainly intellectuals from the Bay Area. Tom had been arrested and charged with conspiracy after the Chicago police riots at the Democratic National Convention in 1968, when Bobby Seale had also been arrested. There were eight defendants in all, and at their trial, Judge Julius Hoffman had ordered Bobby to be tied and gagged. Being the only black among the defendants, plus being the only one to be tied and gagged, it was a clear case of racism at work. When Tom spoke about the incident at the Mitford gathering, David thought he wasn't making that point clear enough, and he became furious, as only he could, or at least as furious as he could be when there was no immediate threat to him. He threw a soda pop bottle at Tom, and in response all the Panthers rose and jumped across the table to take up defensive positions. Genet was one of the first across the table. He was moving, instinctively, with us. My mind was blown and I began seeing him with new eyes. But, frankly, I was most shocked by Hilliard's action in the first place. And he hadn't even hit Tom, who had ducked out of the way. The bottle hit the teenage daughter of one of the guests, right in her face, and as she was screaming and bleeding, I knew we had forever lost the support of anyone we'd hoped to win over that night. Bobby, Ericka, the New York 21, and everybody else needed all the support we could get, and yet there was David, trying to impress everyone, make them think he was a tough guy, but turning everyone off. I never got the chance to find out what Genet thought about it all. The only time we had a private conversation, we were debating what constituted revolutionary art. Running the party line, I argued that it was content that determined whether or not art was revolutionary, while Genet insisted that, no, it was not content but the practice of using a medium in a totally new way that determined whether art was revolutionary. Genet, I would later come to think, was right. His position was the solid one. My position was based on not wanting to be accused of deviationism in case he later repeated our conversation to others. Dogmas and party lines are the enemies of creativity and freedom of expression.

11

Jasmine and Orange Blossoms

On April 16, 1970, my thirty-fourth birthday, I walked into headquarters and recognized a comrade from Baltimore. It had been a long time since I had seen her, so I instinctively began to smile. I stopped when she didn't change her solemn expression. I immediately understood that my time was up. She handed me a cassette. I took it into an office and began listening. The police in Baltimore had found a skeleton and identified it as the agent sent into the party and last heard of the summer of 1969. Now, they were contacting Panthers and offering them immunity in exchange for their testimony on behalf of the prosecution. They even went so far as to name those who were going to be charged with kidnapping and murder. When the person on the tape started reading the list of those who would be arrested, the first name was mine. I immediately shut the tape off, gave it back to the comrade, told her to get it to our lawyer, Charles Garry, and disappeared.

Finally, I was free! I had written my resignation letter to Huey the month before, but hadn't sent it to him because I hadn't figured out how to avoid the wrath of the Panther paper and those on the central committee who wanted me offed. But now I could avoid all that. The Baltimore case had freed me. There was no doubt now: I would go to Algiers and join Eldridge.

Within hours of hearing my name on that cassette, I was into my long-thought-out disguise. The only thing I needed was a new passport. I decided to wait and see how the case developed. I didn't want to get the passport until the last minute before I left. That way, if the authorities caught on and discovered who I really was, I would already be gone.

After dark, I walked up and down Fillmore Street to see if people would recognize me in my disguise. When I passed in front of the Panther office, the comrades gave no sign of recognition. I even locked eyes with some of the people I was living with and they didn't recognize me. That gave me the necessary confidence in my disguise. If even they couldn't recognize me, then surely the authorities wouldn't when I went down to the Federal Building to get my passport. The FBI offices were in the same building.

I contacted headquarters for money that would allow me to move when necessary. June Hilliard told me to stop acting crazy and come back to work, and Garry said the cassette was nothing to be alarmed about. I was enraged. They knew about my predicament. I had sent a report immediately after the Baltimore incident, and I just couldn't believe they were now so blinded by their paranoia that they couldn't deal with my reality. I had to have money, so I went to headquarters to argue my case in person. I was furious I was forced to blow my disguise, even though it was only in front of a few people.

I signaled to enter as I usually did and started climbing the stairs to the second floor of the Berkeley headquarters. As I turned to go up the last stairs, Eddie Griffin looked down and, mistaking me for a stranger, moved back to take some defensive action. I had to start talking fast to make him recognize me. That was a close call. My disguise worked almost too well.

As it turned out, I blew my disguise for nothing. The only thing I accomplished was getting David to decide to have a meeting at Garry's pad the next day. At that meeting, they finally let it sink in that there might be reason for me to lie low for the moment, and they agreed to send someone to Baltimore to investigate the contents of the cassette.

I laid up and waited for the next two weeks. Finally, I heard on the news that the bust had started and the authorities were looking for me. I immediately went to the Federal Building and applied for a passport, wearing my disguise and using the identity of my childhood friend. I said I had to catch a plane to Europe the next day for a business conference, and the clerk said my passport would be ready the next morning. I sent a friend to pick it up, since I didn't want to risk discovery. The only problem now was money. I called June again and he said they would move on it. I couldn't wait, however, and contacted my comrades in the Newsreel film collective and was given money on the spot. I then drove to Los Angeles.

I wanted to book a flight to London, but the first thing open wasn't until Sunday afternoon, and it was only Friday. There was nothing to do but wait, even as uptight as I was. On Sunday morning around ten o'clock, I received a phone call from June telling me they had the money. I told him to keep it and hung up.

I only booked my escape as far as London; I didn't want to plan all the way through to Algiers, thinking that might attract attention. Checking in at the airport, I was shaky, to say the least; there was just no way of knowing if the authorities were on to me or not. The only thing to do was try to be as cool as possible. The officials hardly looked at me. As the plane lifted off the runway, I allowed myself to relax for a few minutes. Then I had to think about the next step. Once I was in London, I knew I would have to stay inside the transit area and not risk going through customs again. Transit was international territory and I couldn't be touched there.

After arriving at Heathrow Airport, my next task was to find a ticket counter inside the transit area so I could book a flight to Paris. I wasn't even sure such a thing existed, but fortunately it did and I didn't have to go through customs. When I made it to Paris, all that was left was getting through customs without being stopped. Upon entering the terminal building at the Orly airport, I immediately recognized the agents who had held me up the last time. Even though I was confident in my disguise, I kept potted plants, support pillars, and anything else I could between me and them. I got through customs with no problems and headed for Ellen Wright's Paris pad.

Ellen telephoned Eldridge for me. He would need to know the name and number on my new passport so he could get the Algerians to clear my arrival at the airport there. The Algerian authorities didn't allow Americans in their country without first getting a visa from an Algerian embassy or consulate in a foreign country, and that took too long, so we were hoping Eldridge could use his connections to help us get around that. It was difficult communicating with Eldridge because Ellen didn't want to use my real name and so he didn't know who she was talking about. Finally, he understood this was about helping someone in trouble and he agreed to put in the clearance. Going back through Orly was the same tense experience as coming in; I saw the same faces as before and I just buried my head in a newspaper until my flight took off.

Dar El Beïda sure looked good. Free at last, I could finally start the process of winding down. I received the same welcome as last time, was speedily processed, and finally was at Eldridge's side. He cracked up when he realized the mystery person was me. As we drove to the Pointe, I ran down what had happened.

We had some urgent business to attend to. The last time I was in Algiers Eldridge had asked headquarters to send him some Panthers who could help in the international effort, and I was given authorization to ask Sekou Odinga and Larry Mack if they would like to join Eldridge abroad, and they were pleased at the prospect. They had been underground for about a year, and since there was no underground machinery within the party to help them, their lives weren't too comfortable. They needed a breath of fresh air and, besides, those were two down brothers; Eldridge couldn't have asked for better. We had several meetings trying to figure a way to get them to Algiers, but the only thing we could think of was to hijack a plane. I urged Sekou and Larry to stay away from Cuba at all costs, given the problems Byron Booth and Rahim Smith had had when they had hijacked a plane to join Eldridge in Cuba in 1969, but there must have been some problem because they arrived in Havana, coincidentally on the same day I arrived in Algiers. As I had warned them, they soon encountered problems with the Cubans, and we had to move fast to get them out.

We got the necessary clearance from the Algerian authorities and communicated that to the Cuban embassy. We also gave the Cubans a letter to deliver to Sekou and Larry, who we figured were being detained. Days went by, and then weeks. Still no Larry and Sekou. Finally, at one of our many inquiries at the Cuban embassy, they gave us a letter from our comrades. It was obvious from the contents that they had never received our letter. We couldn't figure out what game the Cubans were playing, but now at least we knew our comrades were okay.

Two months later, we heard that there were two black Americans going around Algiers looking for Eldridge. We knew it was Sekou and Larry, but we couldn't figure out why they hadn't just come to the house, not knowing the consul assigned to meet every flight from Cuba to Algiers had instead avoided them and refused to take them to Eldridge or give them his phone number. We went to town and started searching, finally spotting them. After all the hugging and hand slapping was over, they explained why they had ignored my advice and gone to Cuba. What they couldn't explain was why the Cubans had held them there for two months. They had been treated well and had a constant security guard and a vehicle at their disposal, but all that had cost the Cubans money, which made it even harder for us to understand why they had been held for so long when they'd had authorization from the Algerian authorities to release them the first day they'd arrived.

That was a disagreeable chapter, to say the least.

Within a few days after I arrived in Algiers, a reporter spotted me riding around with Eldridge, and soon Eldridge was bombarded with phone calls from journalists all over the world asking if Rap Brown was staying at his place. Rap was the party's minister of justice and had gone underground to avoid some charges that meant big time, and the reporters were disappointed when they learned it was only me, the party's field marshal. I wasn't good copy.

It's worth mentioning that the Algerian authorities really showed solidarity with our struggle in the States by welcoming us the way they did. The day after I arrived, Eldridge took me down to present me to the authorities in charge of liberation movements, and they immediately gave me the identification card that was issued to all representatives of liberation movements, plus a new passport. That was real solidarity.

The first weekend I was there, the North Korean embassy invited us to attend some diplomatic function. Eldridge didn't feel like going and asked me to go instead. The gathering reminded me of the time I'd been invited to tea with the president of San Mateo Junior College; I felt out of place, and this time I didn't even speak the language. I couldn't talk to anyone, and I passed the evening standing up, looking like an idiot with hands behind my back, sweating like a racehorse. I was miserable. After a time, relief came in the form of a representative of the Zimbabwe African People's Union. Zimbabwe was still a British colony, so he spoke English, and I was happy to have someone to talk to before he had to move on and greet other people. The diplomatic circuit is rather interesting. Not only does everything you do have a meaning, but everything you don't do does as well. For example, if you don't greet someone, that means there is some disagreement between your governments or movements. Not showing up at a function after receiving an invitation is like breaking off diplomatic relations. It became difficult to keep up with it all during the summer season; we were going out five or six nights a week.

As part of forging these diplomatic connections, we had the opportunity to see movies from all over the world, and it was then that I began seeing clearly what Genet had been talking about when we had discussed what made revolutionary art. Some of the films really surprised me. One evening we sat through a movie at the Korean embassy that started off with a village of Koreans sending off delegations on bicycles, accompanied by martial music, flowers, and crowds of residents smiling and waving goodbye. After this scene was shown in one village, the action shifted to another village, also sending off its delegation. In the end, the movie consisted of nothing but village after village after village. For one hour! After about the third village I heard a loud snore and turned to see Eldridge all slumped over the ambassador, snoozing away. The ambassador merely smiled and signaled to let him alone.

Once Sekou and Larry had joined us at the Pointe, we started looking for a house that would be big enough to use as an embassy and living quarters. We looked all over town and finally found a place that was the right size and in a neighborhood that didn't look too bad, so we took it and paid one year's rent in advance. We also needed transportation, so we looked for cars to rent. None were being imported at the time, and the biggest one we could find was a Renault 16. After my GTO, I felt like I was in a Model T Ford, but it seemed to be the best thing available, so we rented two—one for Eldridge and one for the rest of us. Little did we know we had just sown the seed of resentment throughout Algiers. It turned out that the neighborhood where we had rented the house was the most bourgeois neighborhood in the city, and the R16 was the car everyone dreamed of having. We didn't know that, of course; we were using a standard of judgment formed in the States, with no idea how it was making us look to the locals. That's what makes most Americans come off as "ugly Americans" when they travel outside the United States; we only see things through our red, white, and blue filter.

And that was just the beginning of it. The Algerians had more cause to think we were arrogant when we started complaining it was taking longer than a week to get our phone installed. We were used to calling Ma Bell in the morning and having the phone in the afternoon, but we didn't know that this was unheard of outside of the United States. Naturally they thought we were crazy. In Algiers, getting a telephone took months! We made all kinds of mistakes like that at first. By the time we started understanding what we were doing, the damage was done.

Add to all this that American niggers are a special breed of nigger. We were often seen as arrogant and pretentious simply because, not knowing the rules, we did everything for ourselves, like we had been used to doing all our lives. We didn't wait on anyone to do anything for us. We received a stipend of four hundred dollars a month, like all other liberation movements, but we viewed that money as mostly just a symbolic gesture of solidarity (it maybe covered our gas and electricity bill), and so we found other means to pay our own way. We were to discover later that most representatives from other liberation movements had only that amount to live on—period. Some of them also derided us as bourgeois.

The thing that topped the cake occurred two weeks after we paid our year's rent in advance on the house. We were summoned to the Algerian office that was responsible for liberation movements and were told they had decided to give us the former villa of the National Liberation Front of Vietnam, in the El Biar sector of Algiers. The Viet Cong were by then recognized as a government and had been given an entire complex instead of just a villa. Eldridge had been persistently asking for such a place since he had arrived in Algiers, but we thought nothing would ever come from his request because the Algerians usually didn't give such facilities to mere liberation movements; you had to be a government. But lo and behold, we were now being given an embassy. We took that as a sign of the importance of the black struggle inside the United States, and the importance of the role of the Black Panther Party in that struggle.

Kathleen Cleaver was pregnant at this time, and the government of North Korea had invited her to come to Pyongyang to have the baby. After she left, Eldridge and I were invited to the embassy for dinner with the ambassador. Eldridge mentioned that my comrade Barbara was also pregnant and was due to give birth about the same time as Kathleen, and in a couple of days an invitation came for Barbara to go to Pyongyang and join Kathleen. I was pleased. When I had skipped the country, I had left my letter of resignation from the Panthers with Barbara back in the States, and she knew not only how I was feeling about things but had seen for herself all the shit that was going down in the party, too. Here was an opportunity to get her out of the mess.

We were now ready to go to work building the International Section of the Black Panther Party. During the summer of 1970, Eldridge led a delegation of progressive forces from the States to North Korea, and during his absence, Sekou, Larry, Bill Stevens, and I would prepare our embassy to officially open on September 13, when he was scheduled to return. Thanks to my Algerian girlfriend, Djamila, and Eldridge's girlfriend, Malika Ziri, we managed to get the necessary work done and the embassy started taking shape. The authorities were accommodating, and everything went off without a hitch. It was also with the help of Djamila that I discovered some of the beauty of Algiers. A summer night in Algiers, with a full moon and the air perfumed by orange blossoms and night jasmine, will make a romantic of anyone—at least temporarily. And if you can top all that off with some good-quality North African hash, heaven couldn't be better.

My bubble of bliss was burst by a summons from the Algerian authorities and the officials responsible for liberation movements. The body of an American had been found and identified as that of Rahim, one of our comrades. They wanted an explanation. I was uptight, to say the least. I wished they had waited until Eldridge got back. I wasn't there when Rahim was killed and didn't know what had happened, so I could only repeat the report from headquarters, which said that Byron Booth and Rahim had had a dispute with Eldridge, and to finance their departure they had ripped off $50,000 of party funds that had been raised by the support committee in Europe. I repeated that story to the Algerians and heard nothing more about the incident.

12

Acid and Pyramids

The glorious day finally arrived. On August 5, 1970, Huey was released from prison. Now we were going to see the changes we were all waiting for, and things would get back on the road. When Huey had been shot and imprisoned back in October 1967, there were only a handful of people in the Bay Area who called themselves Panthers, but four years later, when he was released, there were thousands of people waiting to greet him outside the Alameda County Courthouse. The party was now not only a national organization but it had an international office as well. And the party was known all over the world.

Huey called us in Algiers and we were bubbling over with enthusiasm. It sure was good hearing his voice again. We all loved brother Huey and would have done anything he asked. We were confident he was going to straighten everything out.

Just two days after Huey was released, seventeen-year-old Jonathan Jackson made a daring raid on a Marin County courtroom and took hostage the judge, a prosecutor, and three women jurors. He demanded the release of the three men, including his older brother George, known as the Soledad Brothers, who had in January of that year been involved in the revenge killing of a guard at Soledad Prison. Jackson offered weapons to the prisoners in the courtroom and three accepted them: James McClain, William Christmas, and Ruchell Magee. When they got into a waiting van to make their getaway, the police opened fire, and the massacre that followed showed just how desperate the authorities were to prevent the success of any revolutionary actions. Ruchell Magee was the only survivor among the revolutionaries, but among the hostages, only the judge, Harold Haley, was killed. Two others were wounded.

Groups across the country had also started engaging in guerrilla activities. There were many mistakes and many comrades getting killed, wounded, or captured. I began to feel a sense of responsibility to share lessons I had learned in similar actions in the past. There were too many people writing books and articles that were nothing more than syntheses of books and articles dealing with guerrilla warfare in other countries and were not based on real experiences of their authors, or real conditions inside the United States. In order to provide some advice based on real conditions and real experiences, I decided to write about an actual operation I had been involved in. That would legitimate the writing. Since I had left the States for good and had no intention of returning, I would sign it with my own name. I started writing.

Around that time, the Algiers group received our daily copy of the *International Herald Tribune* and we were shocked to see a photograph of Eldridge taken at the Pan-African Cultural Festival the year before. The photo accompanied a feature article on the front page that talked about a delegation he was said to be currently leading in the Middle East to visit Palestinian refugee camps. I knew the press distorted information to shape public opinion, but that was the first time I had seen them publish a total fabrication. We immediately contacted the Algerian authorities, the office of the Palestine Liberation Organization, and Panther headquarters in the Bay Area and informed them of this false news story. If there were niggers in the Middle East, we figured they had to be members of the CIA because, as everyone knew, Eldridge was in Pyongyang. Nevertheless, for the next three days, front-page articles appeared about Eldridge and his alleged delegation in the Middle East. Internationally, the stories had no effect, and in the States, all I knew was that Huey had denounced and denied them in a press conference. And yet, thousands of people must have read those articles and thought they were true, and we felt powerless to stop them. The *International Herald Tribune* was jointly published by the *New York Times* and the *Washington Post*, both considered to be reputable newspapers, and it was distributed around the world. The PLO offered regrets about the incident and said they would be sending official invitations so that we really could visit their camps.

Meanwhile in Pyongyang, Kathleen gave birth to a girl, Joju, and Barbara gave birth to a boy, Pyong-zi-Yong. Their names were given by Madame Kim Il-sung, the wife of the leader of North Korea. Understanding how vicious children can sometimes be, and knowing he would have enough fighting to do without having to struggle every day with a name like Pyong-zi-Yong, we changed his birth certificate the instant they returned to Algiers, calling the baby Jonathan Carlos, after Jonathan Jackson and Carlos Marighella, the Brazilian urban guerrilla. If he ever goes back to visit his place of birth, he can be Pyong-zi-Yong there, which means "he who fights the imperialist."

Eldridge was to return to Algiers on Friday, September 11, for the grand opening of the new International Section of the party. While Eldridge was in North Korea, I had asked Malika, his Algerian girlfriend, not to come around anymore, figuring it wasn't good for the party's reputation with our Algerian hosts. She was a very young girl, still in high school, and I knew that the Algerians who were aware of Eldridge's affair were furious. Such a relationship was totally against their traditions and culture and was the cause of much harm in our dealings with them. I felt that the struggle and the party were more important than any personal relationship, so I tried to keep her away.

It was during this time that I started to lose some of my blind admiration for Eldridge. I had never met him before that first meeting at Emory's the day after Huey was shot, and in the months that followed, all I saw of Eldridge was him working like ten men to build a mechanism that would keep Huey from the gas chamber. I never got the chance to know him as an individual, and even over the years I worked beside him, it was always work. So it came as quite a shock when, the day after the opening ceremonies of the International Section in Algiers, he moved all his books and belongings and refused to come to the embassy. I felt a greater shock and a sense of dumbfounded disappointment when he explained that if Malika couldn't come round, he wasn't coming round. I thought there had to be more to it than that; surely he couldn't be putting a sixteen-year-old girl before the struggle and the party.

Sekou, Larry, Connie Matthews, Bill Stevens, and myself carried on the functioning of the embassy without him, hoping he would soon come to his senses. We didn't expose what was going on to anyone outside because we felt that the struggle and the party were more important than that kind of petty bullshit. That was one of the biggest mistakes we made, and proof we hadn't thoroughly absorbed the struggle against liberalism that we had learned from Mao.

After a time, when it looked like Eldridge was never coming back, we called a meeting and told him to come. He showed up and everyone got on his case. But he had nothing to say about the struggle or the party. He only talked about his relationship with Malika. It turned out he was uptight not only because she had been told not to come around but also because she had had an affair with Larry during the summer. It was during this meeting that we also questioned Eldridge about Rahim's death. We wanted to know why only Rahim was killed if supposedly both he *and* Byron had ripped off the money. He answered sarcastically that he needed Byron to help him bury Rahim. But by that point we had learned that Rahim had had an affair with Kathleen, so we asked Eldridge whether that had anything to do with his choice to kill Rahim but not Byron. He became very uptight. "Yes! I killed the motherfucker. The minute he fucked Kathleen he was a dead man."

He started ranting and raving about his wife and how he would "kill any motherfucker" who dared touch his wife. As I was seeing and hearing all this, I was watching one of my idols crumble into dust. Something inside me was torn apart, for all time. Flashes of things I had heard in the past started resurfacing in my memory. I remembered Emory saying, "The man's crazy." But if that was so, why hadn't the party leadership given any details so that we all could have known? We had just opened the international embassy, but really, this was the beginning of the end. And we were stuck. Only Connie and Bill had real passports, while Sekou, Larry, and I were stranded, thousands of miles from home, without legitimate papers. Sekou and Larry had even gone so far as to hijack a plane in order to come work with Cleaver, and now they were in this mess.

There was no need to call headquarters. Some crazy things were going on over there, too. Huey had become the "Supreme Commander" and was driving around in a Cadillac and living in a penthouse. All communication with Algiers was cut, and the only person authorized to communicate with us was

Huey himself. If anyone was caught contacting us they were severely punished. It must have been serious. We didn't even get anonymous letters. People must have been really terrified.

And for those of us abroad, Cleaver had become mortal in our eyes and we now considered him to be a sick person. Still, though, we kept it a secret; we couldn't see any benefit to publicly exposing all we had learned. With things getting out of control at headquarters, it felt even more necessary for us to stick together and try to find out what was going on and decide what we were going to do.

It wasn't long before we received orders that we were to convince the entire international community that the Supreme Commander had decided the party would no longer embrace internationalism but something Huey called "intercommunalism." Then, the next thing we knew, Huey was no longer the Supreme Commander but the Supreme Servant of the People. It looked like whatever it was that Eldridge had was catching, and Huey had caught it, too.

We decided to send Connie Matthews back to headquarters to find out what was going on and then report back to us. But after she arrived in the Bay Area, we never heard from her. And phone calls from Huey were coming less and less frequently. We didn't know what was going on.

Around that time, we heard on the news that the psychologist and writer Timothy Leary had escaped from a California prison, where he had been serving a long sentence for possession of marijuana. Eldridge and I had once met him on a flight from New York to San Francisco, and he seemed to be a likeable person. A couple of days after we'd heard of his escape, someone came to Algiers asking if we would allow Leary to join us. There wasn't really much to discuss; he was more or less a symbol to many activist progressive whites, and his presence would be a chance to tighten up our solidarity. Besides, he had been sprung from prison by the Weathermen, the most advanced element of the white radical movement, and the one we felt closest to. Within twenty-four hours after we agreed, Leary arrived with his wife, Rosemary.

We presented them to the Algerian authorities and told them that Leary and Rosemary were now part of our group. They didn't know about Leary and his history of promoting psychedelic drugs, so things went fine. After they read his resumé, which included teaching at Harvard, they even wanted to give him a job at the university in Algiers.

We passed long hours listening to Leary recount his escape. He loved an audience, so he gave a good performance. But after listening to him for a while it was obvious that, in addition to Cleaver, we now had another "patient." As far as Leary was concerned, acid would save the world. For him, there was no other way.

Leary's birthday was in a couple of weeks, so it was decided we would have representatives from the movement come over from the States and hold a press conference to announce his presence in the International Section of the Black Panthers. The delegation included Marty Kenner of our New York support committee and Jennifer Dohrn, the sister of Weathermen leader Bernardine Dohrn. When the press conference was announced, however, we didn't realize the impact it would have. We announced the presence of Timothy Leary and a "Miss Dohrn," but without indicating it would be Bernardine's sister instead of Bernardine herself, and the news went off like a bomb.

Suddenly, every Algerian embassy and mission around the world was flooded with demands from journalists for visas, and they converged on Dar El Beïda airport. The Algerian authorities were totally unprepared and, not really understanding what was going on, they told us to take Leary to the pad at the Pointe and keep him out of sight. They then confiscated all the cameras and recording equipment of the journalists who were piling up at the airport, and only then let them enter the country. The authorities ended up with a mountain of equipment; they had never seen anything like it. Naturally, they decided to run a quick check to find out who this Timothy Leary person actually was and why he was getting so much attention. When they found out, they weren't too pleased. They held some hurried meetings to decide what to do.

The first thing was to cancel the press conference. That step would be necessary in order to lift the media siege at the Algerian embassies and missions around the world; they just couldn't deal with the flood of demands for visas. More important, but only implied, they didn't want to be seen supporting Leary's acid philosophy. The decision came down that Leary would be taken to another country, surfaced there publicly to take the heat off Algiers, and then, after about a week, brought back into the country, when, with luck, everything would be cool.

Arrangements were made for us to take Leary to the Middle East and surface him in one of the Palestinian camps. We were given four round-trip tickets to Beirut. Just like old times, it was decided that this was a job for the field marshal to handle. There were no direct flights to Beirut, so we flew to Cairo and laid over two days. I was pleased to have the opportunity to visit Egypt, the cradle of civilization, the land of the pharaohs.

We arrived in Cairo with no problems. We asked the taxi driver to take us to a good but inexpensive hotel, and he drove us to a hotel called the Omar Khayyam. It was the palace built by King Farouk to receive all the heads of state for the opening of the Suez Canal, and it looked like it hadn't been touched since then—the same furniture, everything. It was like something on a Hollywood movie lot: huge rooms with high ceilings filled with Louis XVI–style furniture. It was the kind of fantasy that was perfect for lodging the "Acid King," Miss Dohrn, Marty Kenner (who resembled a plump Woody Allen), and me, Field Marshal DC. We played queen and kings for a day.

While Jennifer and I were getting acquainted in our "royal chamber," Leary and Marty disappeared, which got me all uptight since, being responsible for their security, I didn't want to have any mishaps. Cairo was a huge city, and with everyone and his brother having agents there, it seemed fairly easy to disappear and never be heard from again. Finally, they showed. Leary had wanted to go sightseeing. Even though he was traveling with a false passport, he apparently felt free as a bird and seemed convinced that he was invincible. One thing was sure: they felt more secure than I did. President Nasser had died just a couple of months before, and I wasn't so sure about the new regime. The four of us were attracting enough attention as it was, and I advised that we stick together until we got back to Algiers.

From Cairo, we boarded a flight to Beirut and arrived in the early evening. In Algiers, the authorities had asked me to travel unarmed, saying that when the PLO representatives met us in Beirut, they could supply me with whatever I wanted. So, for the first time in a long time, I was traveling naked. And Leary was making me nervous. On the flight, Leary satisfied his need for an audience by striking up a conversation with some stranger. I just couldn't get him to be cool.

As soon as we walked into the terminal to go through Lebanese customs, I began to feel uptight, especially seeing all the police carrying M16s. To me that indicated they had relations with the Americans. I immediately felt that we were on enemy territory. Plus, there didn't seem to be anyone waiting for us. And there I was without a piece. Of course Leary was entirely content. It was well known at that time that one of Lebanon's government ministers was one of the biggest hash producers in the world, so Leary must have felt like we were in friendly territory, but with all those M16s, I was convinced otherwise. After looking around for our contacts, we decided we couldn't just stand around waiting all night, so we took a taxi to the St. Georges Hotel.

While we were waiting for room service to bring dinner, I called Eldridge in Algiers to let him know something wasn't going right. I told him that no one had met us at the plane, and I asked him to check with the Algerian authorities to see what was going on. We decided that first thing the next morning I would go to PLO headquarters and try to find someone who was supposed to be dealing with us. I had been given one name as a contact. We finally went to bed, but it was difficult to sleep because someone was banging on a typewriter all night in the room next to ours.

After a breakfast fit for a king, I went to PLO headquarters. No one knew anything about us or the whereabouts of the person I asked for. I'd been burnt before, so I got the picture right away. The only thing they could suggest was that I return to the hotel and, when the person I was looking for showed, they would have him call us.

We had been had. It was then clear to me that the so-called trip to the Palestinian camps was just a way to get us out of Algeria and take the pressure off the Algerians themselves. Now, I never minded being used if I was let in on it and I agreed, but when it was slipped to me dry like that, I got furious. Anything could have happened! I was unarmed, Leary was traveling with a fake passport, and it was obvious from all the American cars and military equipment that Lebanese relations with the United States were more than cordial. Later I was to discover that in apartheid South Africa the Lebanese were classified as honorary whites. I also worried that even if the Lebanese didn't arrest us at the behest of the Americans, they could have busted Leary for the forged passport. I rushed back to the hotel and called Eldridge again and told him to deal with that shit. If something didn't happen soon, I was coming back and Algeria would have to take the heat.

Meanwhile, there was nothing to do but wait. Beirut was beautiful and so was Jennifer. As we were talking, we walked out onto the balcony of our room. We were on the third floor of the hotel, and from our vantage I saw a man in the building across the street looking our way with what appeared to be a telescope. I took him for a voyeur trying to get a peek at Jennifer, who was wearing only a T-shirt, but then as we continued to talk, I leaned over the balcony and saw men crouched everywhere, behind every car and lamppost, anything available, and each one had a telescope. For a second, I wondered if Leary had dropped some acid in my orange juice. Then I saw a man, a camera dangling from his side, climbing up the sewer pipe on the side of a building, and more men on roofs that had views of our balcony. All those men weren't a hallucination; they were photographers. And they were everywhere. As it turned out, the person Leary had talked to on the plane was a reporter, and he had recognized Leary's face. Apparently, the whole Middle East press corps had been looking for us since we arrived, and now they all seemed to be outside our hotel. What's funny is that it took them a while to find us because they never thought to look inside the very hotel that had long been their favorite. That explained the typewriter we had heard all night next door.

Finally, Leary was uptight too. He leaped across his bed and was dressed in a second. Someone opened the door to check out the hallway, and flashes started popping off. We were surrounded—under siege. There was no way out. I knew we were in trouble. With all that attention, it wasn't possible for the Lebanese authorities to ignore us, and I wondered how much time we had. I made another desperate call to Algiers to let Eldridge know about the new situation, and I asked that he try to speed up our rescue.

Marty went downstairs to see what he could find out. He ran into a journalist he knew from New York—a Jew who had married a black woman and then become a Muslim and moved to the Middle East. It seems he was a progressive back home, so we decided to invite him up and see what we could work out.

We learned that there is a code between journalists that says they wouldn't use personal relationships to get scoops on each other. In order for him to be able to continue working among his colleagues, he would have to share at least something with them. I didn't want anything to do with all those vultures who were putting so much pressure on us and jeopardizing our security, but as a group we decided that we would let the journalist interview us and then he could deal with that information the way he liked—in exchange for his helping us, naturally. Our top priority was getting Leary away from that hotel and hidden somewhere. He was running the greatest risk because of his false passport. The journalist left us to see what plan he could come up with.

I asked Marty to go down and see if he could find a journalist I knew—Eric Pace of the *New York Times*, whom I had met at Cleaver's pad in Algiers. He was one of the best-known journalists around the Middle East and knew most of the region's heads of state. Because of his reputation, I thought that if there were anyone around who could give me an assessment of our situation vis-à-vis the Lebanese authorities, it would be

Pace. Marty found him and brought him to the room. I asked Pace what he thought the authorities were going to do. He said that probably the next day someone would show up quietly and ask us to leave. I said, "That's all?" and he answered, "That's all." I relaxed a bit. I was confident he knew what he was talking about. Twenty-four hours would be plenty of time to get out of there, to safety.

The journalist Marty knew came back then, and his plan was to create a diversion so Leary could go out the back door, where the reporter's wife would be waiting with a car to drive him to their house. Leary would lie there until we could get a flight back to Cairo. To draw attention away from Leary's escape, we decided to hold a press conference downstairs in the banquet room that the hotel had put at our disposal. We announced that the purpose of the gathering would be to present Miss Dorhn to the press. At that time they still didn't know that "Miss Dohrn" was not Bernardine but her sister. With that distraction pulling journalists out of the hallway, Leary would then have a chance to slip out of the service elevator and into the waiting car.

At the appointed hour, Jennifer, Marty, and I took the elevator down to the banquet room. For the first time in days, the hallway in front of our room was empty. So far, so good. But as soon as we stepped off the elevator I knew something wasn't right. The photographers and journalists that had been laying siege to our room just looked at us as we went by and didn't seem to be particularly interested. We entered the banquet room, in which we found only a couple of TV teams and a handful of journalists. Just as we were getting seated and preparing to start the conference, it became clear what was happening. I heard a loud roar of voices and running feet, like a stampede, out in the hallway. I knew then that either the journalist had betrayed us or our room had been bugged. Whatever the case, it was obvious that they were on Leary's trail. At that point, though, there wasn't much to be done about it, so we went ahead and gave the press conference and talked about political prisoners back home and expressed the solidarity of our movement with the struggling people of Palestine, hoping at least some good would come of the event. During the question-and-answer period, Eric Pace of the *New York Times* kept pushing me to denounce the PLO for treating us as they had (I had told him what had happened), but I didn't go for it. Even though I was furious with the way things had been handled, my solidarity with their struggle was stronger than my personal anger.

After the press conference, we returned to our room and waited for news. It came in the form of Leary, worn out and limp as a wet rag, arriving with all the journalists on his tail. He explained that he had taken the service elevator as planned, but when it arrived on the ground floor and the door opened, the reporters were all there waiting for him. He hopped into the waiting car and was then chased through the streets of Beirut. When he finally got to the apartment building of Marty's journalist friend, his wife, the driver, was practically in a state of shock. As they ran into the building, she pointed Leary to a door. He burst in only to find he was in the home of a Lebanese family that was sitting on the floor having dinner. The journalists were right on his heels, so he started opening doors in their apartment and finally found himself trapped in the bathroom—cornered like a rat. When the journalists got to him, he was standing on the toilet, holding onto the pipes, trying to catch his breath. The photographers clicked away. After he got back a little wind, he somehow made it through the pack of journalists, ran back outside, and made his way back to the hotel. The only thing we could do then was wait until three or four in the morning and hope we could sneak out of the hotel and get to the airport while everyone was sleeping. There was a flight at six in the morning and we needed to be on it.

We all staggered up around four in the morning, looked out into the hallway, saw it was clear, and checked out of the hotel. Marty had arranged for a taxi to be waiting for us, and we piled in and told the driver to circle around through Beirut for a while. After we made sure there was no one following us, we told him to head for the airport. Luck was with us and no one seemed to be on our trail. We arrived at the airport, immediately checked in, and hustled our way through customs so that we would be in the transit area, where, in principle, we would be safe.

We had about an hour and a half to kill before the flight, so we looked for a restaurant to have breakfast. The one we found wasn't open yet, but we were allowed to come in anyway, although they could only serve us coffee. We noticed after a while that all the workers in the restaurant kept trying to get a look at us. Marty went to the newsstand and bought one each of all the morning papers, and wouldn't you know, there was Leary, hanging onto the bathroom pipes, under the biggest headlines I'd ever seen, all of them blaring something like THE KING OF HASHISH IN BEIRUT. I guess the Lebanese press had substituted "hash" for "acid" because many people in their culture wouldn't know what acid was. Anyway, all the papers were the same. On the inside pages there were photos of Jennifer, Marty, and myself at the press conference. I guess there wasn't much news that day, because we were about the only thing they talked about. There was even a photo of Marty, Jennifer, and myself on the front page of the *International Herald Tribune.*

The Algerians had wanted Leary surfaced somewhere else—anywhere besides Algeria—and although it wasn't done according to the plans I had been given, the contract had more than been filled as far as I was concerned. By the time we got back to Algiers, a week would have gone by. I guess the PLO had a good laugh about all that, but I had done my job.

Yet there was still the problem of getting back in the country. We had to fly through Cairo again, and with all the attention we were getting, I didn't know how the Egyptian authorities would react. We decided that when we arrived in Cairo, we would check into the hotel that was located inside the transit area, where we wouldn't be on Egyptian territory.

A few minutes before we were to take the bus to the airplane waiting on the tarmac of the Beirut airport, a journalist got through customs and found us. It was Arnaud de Borchgrave of *Newsweek*. He didn't approach us in a friendly manner, and after all the pressure the journalists had put on us over the past few days, we were furious and didn't want to have anything to do with him. When it was time to go to the plane, the airport authorities sent a special bus for just us four, but Borchgrave jumped on also, hoping to get some info out of us. We refused to talk to him. I stared straight into his eyes with the meanest look I could muster. I really wanted to wring his neck. At last, we got on the plane and were off to Cairo.

In Cairo we had to walk from the plane to the terminal, and the distance was far enough that we couldn't distinguish what kind of people were making up the large crowd gathered outside the terminal doors. From where we were, I thought it was passengers waiting to be taken to a flight, but as we drew closer and it became possible to distinguish individuals, I saw that there in the middle of the crowd was Borchgrave. He must have flown there in a military jet; there was no other way he could have gotten to Cairo before us. We had left him on the tarmac at the Beirut airport, and no other commercial flights to Cairo were scheduled, and yet here he was, surrounded by Egyptian soldiers, policemen, officials in civilian clothes, and journalists.

I told my crew to push through the crowd and run into transit. I was surprised when no one resisted us, and, feeling all right, I went into my act. I demanded to see the North Korean, Chinese, and Vietnamese ambassadors. Some official in civilian clothes came to me and said everything was okay, brother, you're on friendly territory and there's nothing to worry about. With that, I turned to Marty and told him to tell the Egyptian authorities that for Borchgrave to have beat us here, he must be working for the CIA. The Egyptian police then proceeded to escort him onto the plane that was returning to Beirut. Finally, a small victory. After we passed a few hours in the transit hotel, the Egyptian authorities came to us and said they would be honored if we would stay a while and visit Cairo, inviting us to leave transit and go into town. We agreed and returned to the Omar Khayyam Hotel. I tried to call Algiers, but apparently Cairo was using the same phone company that had installed our system in the Algerian embassy, and it would take three days to put a call through to Algiers; I sent a telegram instead.

Our next problem was getting back through the airport in Algiers. The policemen there didn't make any exceptions, even if they knew you; you either had to have a visa or you had to have other authorization from the Algerian authorities, period. Jennifer, Marty, and Leary only had American passports, and if I couldn't get through, we would be blocked at the airport. To eliminate that problem, we went to the Algerian embassy in Cairo, explained our case, and were lucky to each receive a visa from the consul. Only then could we relax and see the pyramids.

We returned to Algiers without incident. Meanwhile, Borchgrave was plotting his revenge. He invented one of the most vicious articles I'd ever seen, and it was run, full page, in *Newsweek*. Once again the press printed an article that was an utter fabrication, from the first letter to the last period. He sure was angry with us and was spitting venom. The PLO representatives again apologized and promised to send us invitations to come visit their camps.

Leary also continued to be more of a problem than we had bargained for. It seemed as if the people moving dope on an international level had decided to make Leary and Algiers a crossroads on their route, and that meant trouble for us. The only way to enter Algerian territory at that time was by getting a visa somewhere, or by going through the Panthers, and since Leary was under our auspices, we had to clear, through the Algerian authorities, all of his friends who came to visit. We would meet them at the airport and, for security reasons, search their luggage. We routinely discovered enormous quantities of acid stashed away. If Algerian customs officials ever found any of that stuff, we were all in for it. Talking to Leary was like talking to a brick wall, however, because he was so spaced out he either didn't understand the danger to us or didn't care. Week after week, the pile of confiscated acid grew larger. Leary and Rosemary went so far as to make trips down south to the oasis at Bou Saâda, where the Sahara Desert began, to do their drugs in peace. They would spread out an oriental carpet, strip naked, and drop acid. They were even less concerned for the customs and traditions of the country than we had been.

One day in January 1971 we learned that Leary and Rosemary were planning a dinner party and that among the invited guests, unbeknownst to the Learys, were some agents from the Algerian secret service. It was around five in the afternoon when we were informed, and the dinner was scheduled for eight. We couldn't allow the Algerian authorities to hear Leary run his acid philosophy and possibly be offered a sample; we had to stop the dinner. There wasn't time to convince Leary to cancel it—there were only a couple of hours to go and guests would be arriving soon—so we decided instead to bust Leary and Rosemary and put them under house arrest at our pad at the Pointe. Larry, Sekou, and I went to take them into custody.

When Leary opened the door, he knew immediately that it wasn't a friendly visit and started calling for help. Rosemary was cutting some onions with a long butcher knife, and she gave it up without a fuss. We took them to the car and headed for the Pointe. On the way, Leary showed another aspect of his character when he turned to Rosemary and said, "It's okay, honey; it's just a bunch of niggers flexing their muscles." Obviously he didn't know enough about Sekou, who was sitting next to him. As soon as he heard Leary's words, Sekou made him understand he had made a big mistake.

Once we were at the Pointe, we put the couple on ice. They had all the comforts and didn't suffer any physical neglect, but we held them for about a week, and during that time we filmed them for a video Eldridge wanted to make and send to the States. The soundtrack was a statement by Eldridge that attacked drugs in the movement. In a press release he said, "Something's wrong with Leary's brain....We want people to gather their wits, sober up, and get down to the serious business of destroying the Babylonian empire....To all those of you who looked to Dr. Leary for inspiration and leadership, we want to say to you that your god is dead because his mind has been blown by acid." Unfortunately, the message landed like a stink bomb. Without knowing what had led up to such a drastic position, the progressive movement and many of our allies flew into an uproar. We were branded fascists and pigs. Even the Algerians were on our case.

After we released the Learys, we were summoned by the Algerians to explain ourselves. They said we couldn't create a state within a state. Eldridge asked for a thirty-minute break in the discussion and went out and got all the confiscated acid—enough for twenty thousand hits—and came back and dumped it on the desk of Commandant Slimane Hoffman, the official in charge of liberation movements. With that, the meeting came to a speedy conclusion and we were relieved of the responsibility of the Learys. That suited us fine and ended a very unpleasant episode.

13

Camels and Cadillacs

By then, it was obvious to those of us in Algiers that Huey was not going to straighten out and put things back on the road as we had expected. He had actually reinforced Hilliard's hand and not only continued the backward movement but shifted it into high gear. Geronimo Pratt, a high-ranking member of the party, had been busted in Texas and was then expelled after being accused of wanting to assassinate Hilliard and Newton. The New York 21 were also expelled for criticizing the leadership and politics of the party. There seemed to be a move to eliminate the most radical elements of the Black Panthers.

I had been hoping that Huey would call for a general retreat or something that would allow the party to devise new strategies and tactics to deal with the situation that then existed. Instead, it looked like he was moving on all people who didn't agree with him and his direction—a direction that was in no way clear to us, mostly because it hadn't been defined. I didn't know what to do.

When Huey was released in August of 1970, our love for him was so great that we would have done anything he said. But with the case of megalomania he came out of prison with, his attitude, as far as we could see, was out of sight, out of mind. He kept us isolated and in the dark about what was going on.

About that time I received an anonymous letter—the only one we had ever received—saying, "It's too bad about poor Fred," and then it went on to talk about how messed up things were. It was later revealed, as a result of the Freedom of Information Act, that the letter had been sent by the FBI. I guess the bureau didn't realize how isolated we were and that we didn't even know about the murder of party captain Fred Bennett. When I received the letter, we could only wonder "Fred who?" and "Fred what?" But thanks to their letter, we knew something had happened; the dialectic can be found in the most unusual places.

We began holding meetings with everyone in Algiers to discuss all the problems that we could identify or recognize, with the purpose of deciding what each of us would want to do. Everyone talked of their own experiences. There were so many people in Algiers by that time that after one week we hadn't yet finished hearing from everyone.

Our meetings were interrupted by an invitation of two round-trip tickets from the PLO to attend an international conference on Palestine that was going to be held in Kuwait. Since I was supposedly the Middle East specialist, I was charged with going to the conference and taking with me whoever I wished. I chose Sekou. The only problem was that we both were wanted by the Americans. We were to travel with the PLO representative and other invited guests from Algiers, but the flight plan called for us to pass through Rome, which made us uptight. We knew nothing about the politics of Italy, so when we arrived at the airport, Sekou and I stayed in transit during the layover, with our backs to the wall so that we could watch in all directions. We made it through with no problems and finally left for Kuwait.

It was with great surprise that when the doors of the plane

were opened we were greeted by the spectacle of a Cadillac Eldorado driving up to the disembarking ramp. There was a brother behind the wheel with one of those things on his head like we had always seen Yasser Arafat wear, only he had it broken back in a real mean manner, very cool. For a minute I was wondering if maybe we were at 125th Street and 7th Avenue with the black nationalists in their traditional garb.

Kuwait was a mindblower. The oil that is the country's source of wealth only began to be exploited in the fifties, and that wealth was spread among a population of only about four hundred thousand. All public services were free—schools, hospitals, telephones, utilities, you name it. And as far as housing was concerned, they had some houses that could have served as models for a Cecil B. DeMille movie. Their wealth had not come from the traditional system of exploitation and oppression of one class by another, however, and instead of neighborhoods, and society in general, being organized along class lines, everything was organized along clan and family lines. A sheik's palace might be next door to an ordinary house that was the home of a relative. They didn't seem to have the usual capitalist mentality.

But they also weren't afraid of showing their wealth. It was as if you took a half million niggers from any ghetto and gave them more money than they could spend. Everybody had big rides and pads. Anytime they needed something, they imported the best of whatever it was from wherever it existed in the world. I read an article in a newspaper a couple of years later talking about the number-one social problem of the Kuwaitis, which was...leisure! It turns out they didn't know what to do with all their spare time. While I was there, I remember getting a ride from someone who apologized because his car was already one year old. Even so, the citizens there had a certain comportment that reminded me of brothers off the block, who would stop their cars in the middle of the street, lie back on the fenders and hoods, and rap to each other, all the while fingering their prayer beads. It beat smoking cigarettes.

The other side of the coin was less brilliant. Because of Kuwait's riches, people immigrate there from all over the world seeking jobs. There is a larger immigrant community than there are native Kuwaitis, and it is the immigrants who do all the work. And nothing is free for them. Immigrant workers, I learned, didn't even get social security, which means no sick leave or health benefits. So even though Kuwait's citizens are well provided for and don't lack anything, it's a different story for the immigrant workers.

At the conference, I met a woman, Najat, who worked for local television. She was one of the most intelligent and beautiful people I've ever known. After leaving the studio where she had interviewed me, we met her boss, who was walking with some other men. Also accompanying us was a man who worked as Najat's assistant. I learned something new about Kuwaiti culture when I noticed Najat was talking to her boss while facing her assistant, who then turned to the boss and repeated everything Najat had just said, as if he were her interpreter. It took me some time to realize that she, being a woman, didn't have the right to speak directly to a man in a higher position. After they finished talking, I asked her how she could deal with that, especially with her intelligence and consciousness. She turned to me and said, "What would you have me do, go to Europe and live like a European?" I tucked my tail between my legs, turned as red as I possibly could, and shut my mouth. Even though she had been educated in the finest schools the western world had to offer, she was home in Kuwait and had no intention of leaving.

Sekou and I were placed in a suite in the new Sheraton hotel, where the conference was being held. Given the accommodations accorded us, it was obvious we were considered something special. It was rather embarrassing comparing our suite to the rooms of those we had traveled with, but we didn't let it bother us too much and settled down to the business of the conference, which, for Sekou, partly meant making friends with the attendees. Sekou and his charm quickly became the pet of all the Palestinian women, and any time you saw a large group of women giggling and talking in a circle, if you could work your way to see what the attraction was, in the center was Sekou. For the women, he was the hit of the conference, and before it was over, they were all calling him by name. They *loved* Sekou.

Finally, it was my turn to deliver the speech that we had prepared back in Algiers. The conference was being held in February of 1971, and only five months before, King Hussein of Jordan had turned his Bedouin army loose on the Palestinians and in a matter of days had massacred twenty thousand of them in an atrocity that came to be known as Black September. During the conference, we were taken to hospitals to see survivors recovering from their wounds. We met some who had been in hospitals in Jordan, including hospitals that had been attacked by King Hussein's troops. Some of the survivors had been wounded twice: once in battle and the second time in the hospital. Not many lived to tell about it.

In my speech, I condemned King Hussein without mincing words. To us he was a butcher and as much an enemy of the Palestinian struggle as Israel. To my shock, I received condemnations for the speech, even by representatives of the PLO. I just didn't understand anything anymore. They told me I shouldn't have said those things about Hussein. He was their brother. The only thing I could think to say was, "With a brother like that, you don't need any enemies."

Before delivering the speech, I had given interviews to print and radio journalists who were covering the conference. None of those interviews were ever published or aired; everything I said was censored. This was a politics that was beyond my comprehension. I didn't understand how I was supposed to be on the side of people who weren't struggling for the same freedoms. For example, I could not consider Idi Amin, the new self-proclaimed president of Uganda, my brother when he was a butcher. Objectively, I understood that he was a product of British colonialism, but subjectively, as far as I was concerned he was also part of the disease inherited from colonialism that must be torn from the body of Africa if the continent is ever to become healthy and whole again. He and all of his kind, like the French creation known as Emperor Bokassa of the Central African Republic, belong on the dung heap of history. The fact that their skins were black didn't cut any ice with me. I considered them my enemies and enemies of freedom and justice.

After the conference ended, Najat took us on a tour to show us Kuwait and a bit of the desert. It was astonishing to see a big patched-up Bedouin tent with sheep, goats, and camels grazing out front and a big Coupe de Ville parked alongside. It was also interesting to meet Kuwaitis whom I had run across at different universities back in the States and who had since finished their studies and returned home. I saw several who had attended San Francisco State College. After a memorable ten days, Sekou and I headed back to Algiers.

We flew from Kuwait to Cairo, and again we made the pilgrimage to the pyramids, which struck me as a Disneyland-type of attraction rather than what you would expect at an ancient historical site. There was a blacktop road that passed the Sphinx, climbed the hill, and circled the biggest pyramid of Cheops before continuing on past the two smaller pyramids. Right in front of the Sphinx there was a restaurant with a huge marble patio in front. With all those millennia of history embodied in these monuments of antiquity, I thought it sacrilege to desecrate the area like that. Perhaps one day someone will see the necessity of removing all those distractions, including those terrible dudes with the camels who hustle tourists to take rides and have their pictures taken. They don't take no for an answer, and I had to walk a good way into the desert to try to shake one. I just wanted to contemplate the historical significance of everything around me without the interference of the modern world, but he wouldn't let me. There was nothing to do; he relentlessly kept trying to convince me to take a ride on his camel. On my return, when we were getting close to the point where we had started and he realized that I really wasn't going to take a ride, he started insulting me and my ancestors, all the way back to Adam and Eve. Apparently, he wasn't used to losing a client.

It was during that trip to Cairo that we met David Du Bois and his mother, Shirley Graham Du Bois. It was a great honor to meet the family of W. E. B. Du Bois. (The great activist became David's stepfather when the younger Du Bois was in his mid-twenties.) We also had the opportunity to spend an evening with a group of Nigerian students who were attending the American University in Cairo. I welcomed the chance to have them clarify for me the Biafran civil war that had just ended in their country, but, unfortunately, each student had a different explanation and the evening deteriorated to the point that it seemed the war was going to be fought over again in the very room we were sitting in.

I left Cairo more confused than ever.

14

The Split

We arrived in Algiers in time to hear a phone call from Huey to Eldridge, coming with the news that the next morning Huey was going to be on a San Francisco television talk show, live.

Since rumors had begun to circulate that he and Eldridge were no longer seeing things eye to eye, he told Eldridge to expect a call while he was on the air. He invited Eldridge to use this opportunity to show the audience that the party was unified and that there were no problems between these two leaders. Eldridge agreed. When he hung up the phone and turned toward everyone in the room, it was understood by all, without a word being said, that this was it. Although our meetings had not yet finished and no decision had been made about what we were going to do, we knew that with Huey calling on live TV, we couldn't allow ourselves to give anyone the impression that we were going along with so many things Huey was doing that we were opposed to. Really, Huey forced our hand here.

At that time, still not having full information about what was going on, I was nevertheless prepared to participate in a leadership retreat to try and devise new strategies and tactics to deal with the existing situation. But, knowing that comrades were going to be watching the show, I couldn't pretend that things were okay between us, that there were no internal contradictions. I voted, along with everyone else in Algiers, to use the occasion to let the world know that we didn't agree with what was going on at headquarters. There was not one dissenting vote. Our hand had been called.

When Sekou and I returned to Algiers, our group had grown. Among the new arrivals were Charlotte and Pete O'Neal from Kansas City, Missouri. Pete was an excellent electrician and had connected the phones to a mechanism that activated tape recorders whenever a handset was lifted. He also hooked up the phones to speakers located throughout the embassy. That way, everyone could get news at the same time. If someone needed to have a private conversation, there was an override switch that cut everything off, but because we were so numerous, and in order to help us not forget anything, all phone calls were recorded. That way, if someone was out, they could listen to what had been said while they were gone. One of the characteristics of exile was our insatiable thirst for information.

The next morning, we were all assembled in the office waiting for Huey's call. Eldridge had written a declaration of our position and was ready to deliver it. Finally, the telephone rang. You could have heard a pin drop. Huey's opening conversation with the announcer was cordial and polite, and then the announcer asked Eldridge if he had a statement he would like to make. And Eldridge dropped the bomb. He made it clear that we weren't going along with the things happening at headquarters and said that we thought David Hilliard, as chief of staff, was destroying the party. When Eldridge finished, there were a few seconds of silence and then Huey said something about going before the central committee and then the announcer hung up the phone.

We waited for Huey to call back. We didn't have to wait long. He had literally gone mad; tapes of those telephone conversations are still floating around somewhere as evidence of what happened. His response was not politically motivated but personal and vindictive. He asked to speak to me, wanting to know where I stood. I told him I didn't agree with the direction things were moving. He said, "Okay, I'm going to crush you."

After that, our Algiers group immediately went to work. We made a lot of videotapes, with everyone giving their opinions, and started sending them to the States. We also made one using the tapes of Huey's crazy declarations. In his madness, he related everything to sex, including saying he would come to Algiers and fuck Kathleen and then he was going to fuck the rest of us in our asses. The conversation went on and on like that until he rang off. Another idol had bit the dust. The Supreme Commander had been insulted on live television and his only response was to vow revenge.

Our telephone started jumping off the hook. Journalists from around the world wanted to know what was going on. That was a good thing, because with our isolation in Algiers, the only way to make our views known was through the news media. We made history of a technical nature when one of our videotapes became the first half-inch tape shown on a national channel. Our distribution network was quite efficient, and just twenty-four hours after we had made them, our tapes were already being shown in the States. In February of 1971, video was our most powerful weapon.

Unfortunately, video also put us and our allies in danger. One of several places we dropped our tapes in the States was at the store of Miriam and William Seidler, who owned a children's clothing shop across the street from the Philadelphia branch of the party. The Seidlers were white progressives from way back (they had been notably active in the defense of Julius and Ethel Rosenberg), and when they received our tapes they passed them on to allies who dealt with getting them shown. On March 18, 1971, a man went into the store and shot William. His killer was never caught. I'm not sure if he was ever even searched for. For me, however, there was never any doubt as to who was behind that cowardly murder.

Things in the States were very uptight by this time, especially in the San Francisco Bay Area. The first thing that happened when the split broke into the open was that everyone went for the stashes of arms. Because of the close relationships between people in San Francisco and Oakland, everyone knew about the same main stashes, as well as other places weapons might be hidden. That created a very dangerous situation. And here the cowardly nature of Newton and his followers was to manifest itself again, although not quite yet.

About this time, Connie Matthews and her husband, Michael Tabor, a member of the New York 21, showed up in Algiers. Through them, we were finally able to get inside information about what had been going on. After we had sent Connie to headquarters back in the fall, we had not heard from her since, and now we found out why: she had become Huey's personal secretary. She told us everything. The goings-on at headquarters sounded like a Fellini movie script: cocaine, orgies, beatings, and murders. We also found out what had happened to Fred Bennett.

As the party grew, and as the repression came down, the traditional forms of personal relationships between certain individual Panthers more or less broke down. One never knew whether one was going to be alive tomorrow, or maybe end up in prison or be sent to some far corner of the country. Relationships of a sexual nature were especially short-lived and superficial, happening mostly between people that were in close proximity at any given time. Bobby Seale, for instance, had been in prison several months when Artie, his wife, became pregnant by Fred Bennett. At the time he became a Panther, Fred was a bus driver in San Francisco, and he was among the hardest working and most dedicated Panthers in the San Francisco office. He happened to be present when Huey started beating "Red," the nickname of Geronimo Pratt's wife, Saundra, and as Fred moved to intervene, that was when he got himself in trouble. One was not supposed to ever make a move in the direction of the Supreme Commander. I don't know which of those two things—defending Red or getting Artie pregnant—was used to justify the decision (and maybe it was both), but Fred was murdered and his body was burned and his bones crushed. I was sent a *San Francisco Chronicle* article after his remains were found and identified. The photograph used to illustrate the news story showed one of the largest pieces of bone they had found, placed next to a dime. The dime was the bigger of the two. Fred Bennett, who had dedicated his life to the struggle for peace, freedom, and justice, was killed to maintain the image and dominance of a megalomaniac.

In one of the videotapes we made in Algiers, each of us gave a criticism about something we specifically knew was going on at headquarters. I criticized David Hilliard and Charles Garry for their negligence in the Baltimore affair. They'd had the cassette tape with all the names of the people who were to be arrested, and yet they made no effort to warn them or protect them, and in the end something like seventeen people were arrested because of their negligence. For me, that was inexcusable and criminal. Things had deteriorated to the point that it was no longer a question of politics, per se. It was a question of dominance and maintenance of their power over others, at all cost.

After the split, the Panthers in New York ran out all those

who supported Newton and Hilliard. One day Zayd called me screaming that Robert "Spider" Webb had been killed, and I knew immediately why. Spider had been lured into a trap at 125th Street and 7th Avenue, the crossroads of Harlem where we used to debate the black nationalists, and he'd been shot in the back of the head with a .45 automatic, in broad daylight. That news crushed me, just as Newton had promised. I stood there holding the phone, only able to speak a few incoherent words. When the others in the office saw that I had flipped out, they took the phone from me to deal with it. I sat in the hallway for the next four days and didn't move or talk to anyone. I don't remember where my mind went; I don't remember anything. All I know is that I went out for four days. I just shut everything off. When I came to myself again, I felt nothing but blind rage and hate. There I was, stuck in Algiers, without the means to move, and seeing my closest comrades being picked off, one by one. I felt a rage and a hate deeper than I had ever felt before. Deeper even than what I had felt when those four little girls were blown up in the church in Birmingham—deeper because of my incomprehension at what was the source of such actions. These murders were not coming from the Ku Klux Klan or from the racist police. They were coming from the thing I had dedicated my life to, that I had seen as the means to put an end to so much suffering. And now it had become a monster and was being used to eliminate the best among us. The drive was no longer focused on the struggle for peace and justice but on the need for power and personal recognition. It had been turned inward upon its own. It had become a cannibal.

Comrades in the States decided then that they could no longer sit idly by while Newton was running wild and ordering the murder of our brothers and sisters. It was, however, necessary to respond as much as possible in a political manner, rather than for personal and emotional reasons. An indiscriminate fratricidal war would serve no purpose other than satisfying the thirst for revenge.

For some time, the Panther paper had been used to attack and vilify anyone who had fallen out of favor with Hilliard and Newton, and it was also one of the primary sources of funds. Those of us who had split from the party agreed to attack the paper by destroying the distribution office in San Francisco and its annex in New York. The office in San Francisco was blown up, and the one in Corona, Queens, was burned down. After the fire was extinguished, the bound and bullet-riddled body of Sam Napier, just thirty-two years old, was found in the ruins.

Sam had been there at the beginning of the paper, when circulation was almost entirely local, and he had always worked like ten people to make it happen. As the paper grew along with the organization, it finally reached the point where it was being printed each week in a run of 250,000 copies. It would come from the printers at night and be air-freighted to all the offices and branches throughout the country. Subscriptions were sent out the same night. Sam's bible was Lenin's *What Is To Be Done?*, a pamphlet dedicated to the idea that the people needed to be educated on political ideals in order to stage a successful revolution. Because Sam had always been in charge of the paper, most of its organization and distribution processes were in his head; he was indispensable. Thus, the destruction of the distribution offices and the assassination of Sam were considered an effective response to the violence and murders being perpetrated by Newton and his gang of cutthroats. Evidently, it had an effect, because it ended the violence immediately associated with the split in the party. I recognize, with a heavy heart, that the four people killed as a result of the split—Bill Seidler, Fred Bennett, Spider Webb, and Sam Napier—were all comrades of mine, three of them from San Francisco.

The only thing to do then was leave Algiers, go back to the States, and help deal with the fallout. It was going to take some time, and yet there was no time to waste. Something had to be done—urgently—because there were many people who were now more or less stranded abroad without support. Before I left, however, we wanted to gather as much information as possible, in hopes it would help us devise a new organizational structure to serve our goals of growth, development, and security. Comrades in San Francisco sent a representative to participate in our discussions, and the ideas we debated would then be carried back to the States for further clarification and revision.

We made contact with representatives from all the liberation movements in Algiers that had ever engaged in any form of urban guerrilla warfare. All day, every day, for a week we received representatives from the different struggles. The only ones we didn't get the chance to talk to were the Tupamaros of Uruguay and the Baader-Meinhof group of Germany. Of every group, we asked that they explain their respective organizational structures and describe their strengths and weaknesses. We made copious notes and recordings. After our final meeting, we talked among ourselves and attempted to synthesize all that we had learned toward creating our own mechanism, customized to deal with our own situation, and profiting from the lessons we had learned from other urban guerrilla struggles. Eldridge refused to participate. He said he didn't have any ideas and, frankly, after the incident that had ended in the death of Li'l Bobby, back in 1968, I knew he was telling the truth. I was not surprised. But I also knew that none of us had any ideas either.

I knew the struggle would be a long haul. It wasn't something that was going to happen overnight. The thing to do was take the time to build something solid and real, something that would have a chance to confront real problems and thereby gain the confidence of others and grow. We figured it would require an aboveground organization, but, at the same time, we wanted it to have a clandestine aspect that was structured for maximum security and survival, even while being connected to and drawing its lifeblood from the aboveground mechanism. Many comrades who were already underground didn't have an organized support mechanism and were in an extremely vulnerable position. We knew devising a liaison between the aboveground and the underground would be complicated; the form of a foolproof liaison has yet to be invented, and it has historically been a weak point with all revolutionary movements. We shared these ideas with our Bay Area comrade and he took them all back to San Francisco.

When our ideas were put before the comrades there, that's when the next split took place. The group was divided between those who more or less supported our ideas and those who didn't. Among those who rejected them were to be found some who had decided they didn't want anything more to do with "revolution" and those who were convinced that the time had come to start the war. I don't know to this day which of the comrades supported the ideas we sent over, but the one comment that came back to me from the side that didn't was this: "Fuck DC."

It was at about this time that the New York 21 were finally freed from all those ridiculous charges, and now they were hitting the streets. They immediately issued a statement saying they didn't want anything to do with anyone that was then, or ever had been, connected to headquarters and the central committee of the Black Panther Party. I was torn apart. Given the state of things when they were released, and everything that had led up to what they had endured, it was easy to understand why. But even though I had fought to support them, I had been a member of the central committee, and that meant they didn't want anything to do with me either. They didn't know the details of my current relationship with the party, and I knew it wasn't possible to explain at that time, and anyway, I didn't think they would have listened or cared. Sekou and Larry, on the other hand, were both from New York, and so it was only natural that the New York 21 would ally themselves with comrades they knew and had struggled with. That, then, split up the group in Algiers. I received the blow with silence, and determined then that I'd try to get along with everyone until I could get myself together and leave Algiers. Everyone else was doing the same, but I think I took it especially hard. I hadn't known Larry before Algiers, and we had never become close, but I'd always considered Sekou one of the best comrades I personally knew (except for his attitude toward women). Having Sekou's back turned on me left me feeling alone; the only one I had left was Barbara. But she wouldn't be staying for long. There was nothing preventing her from traveling, and there was nothing more for her to do in Algiers, so she was free to leave and go elsewhere, where she could be more productive.

I realized it was no use trying to convince anyone of anything, at least not from Algiers. If I had any hope of continuing the struggle, it would be a question of whether we could start all over again. I would need to associate myself with a new group and start from scratch, cutting off all communications with everyone else. I was so down, I mostly just wanted to be forgotten. I withdrew from participating in activities at the office and stayed at the Pointe. It was necessary, for my own safety, to get used to being alone and not moving around, so that's what I did. I didn't make an official public announcement of my resignation from the Black Panther Party, mostly because I didn't want to cause any political problems for us in Algiers. No one was prepared to leave yet, so everyone was playing it cool.

Finally, help materialized in the form of a comrade from the Baader-Meinhof group in Germany. I was disappointed to discover that at that time they were more or less moving for action's sake and action's sake alone, meaning there didn't seem to be a concrete strategy behind the actions they took. But they had done an excellent job of analyzing their problem and identifying the enemy, and had even carried out several spectacular actions that captured the world's imagination. But where were the politics behind it? No matter how spectacular an action was, if it didn't serve to raise the political consciousness of large masses of people, and then mobilize them, it would only give the powers that be an excuse to implement more repressive measures on a general scale. And one of the highest, if not *the* highest, priority for gaining the support of large masses of people is justice. Justice must be the driving force. If justice cannot be seen in the design of an action, it will turn people off. We couldn't afford to let that happen.

15

Resignation

On June 2, 1972, while listening to the news, as I constantly did, I heard reports of an airplane hijacking underway in California. Among the hijackers' demands were $500,000 and the immediate release of Angela Davis, who was in prison on charges related to the 1970 Soledad Brothers incident in which Jonathan Jackson and three others were killed. (Two days after the hijacking, she was acquitted when a jury found her not guilty.) My radio was hooked up to a tape recorder, so I switched it on to register the progress of the hijacking in case anyone might be interested in hearing about it the next day. (It was around two in the morning and I didn't think anyone else monitored the news like I did.) The plane finally left the West Coast and landed in New York, where it was being equipped to cross the Atlantic. It was at that point that I began wondering whether or not whoever had taken the plane might be thinking of coming to Algiers. After the plane had begun the crossing it came as no surprise to me when a news flash said that, indeed, it was headed for Algiers. I started making telephone calls to wake everyone and tell them what was going on. Around nine the next morning, the Algerian authorities called and asked that we accompany them to the airport to welcome the plane.

President Boumédiène and the head of the national police were then traveling outside the country, so it was their aides who were handling everything. They were as excited as we were. Our greeting party consisted of Eldridge, Pete O'Neal, Elaine Klein (our liaison with the Algerians), a man named Hussein from Boumédiène's office, and myself. We Panthers went packing very heavy. After all, we didn't know who or what was going to step off the plane and we didn't want to take any chances. When we arrived at the airport with bulges under our clothes, Hussein begged us to put away our weapons. He was sweating and wiping his brow nervously with a handkerchief. But we weren't going for it. He wanted us to go to the plane and assure the hijackers that everything was cool and they could come off the plane without worrying about anything. We, for our part, wanted to be prepared to deal with any eventuality. Security men took us out to the tarmac to wait for the plane, which was only minutes away from touchdown. Just before it landed, whoever had taken the plane had told the control tower that they were Weathermen. Immediately, the security team held us back and said it wasn't our people. They got to the plane before we did and took the $500,000. As the hijackers disembarked, we could see they were a couple: a black man, Roger Holder, and a white woman, Cathy Kerkow. They were taken to the VIP lounge and then we were called in.

I went straight to Holder and asked where the money was. He said the Algerians had asked for it so they could put it in a safe place. I whispered to him that he had made a mistake and that he would never see it again. Everyone was crowding around Holder then, so I went over to where Kerkow was sitting alone, smiling, looking at the growing crowd around Roger. I sat beside her and started asking questions to find out who they were, what organization they were with, et cetera. She turned to me with a dreamy smile and said, "Oh, we're not with any organization or anything. That's my old man. I just came along for the ride so I wouldn't have to stay home worrying about him."

Our people called a meeting, and I went back to the office for the first time in months. The discussion was centered on how to divide up the money, which they figured would be coming to them by way of the Algerians. That $500,000 would be plenty to provide everyone with more than enough to be able to leave Algiers and do whatever each of us wanted, but I told them they were dreaming and that they weren't going to see the money. We needed to be realistic. Algiers was then in negotiations with Washington for some natural gas contracts, and I just couldn't see the Algerian authorities jeopardizing the economic future of their country for $500,000. No one wanted to hear what I had to say, though, so I went back to the Pointe and my radio.

As it turned out, I was right. A few days later it was announced that the authorities had decided to give the money back to the U.S. government. The dollar signs that had replaced the eyes of the niggers at the office crumbled into dust. But they still wined and dined Roger, and kept him away from me and the Pointe, just in case. Not until about a month later, when it finally sank in that they weren't going to see the money, was he allowed to meet me. I was disappointed, to say the least. He was someone who just had a whim one day and hijacked a plane without any clear political ideas; he was just about the best example of a "blippy"—a black hippie—that I'd ever seen. He told me he had worked for the FBI at one time. And with that, any possibility of a relationship with Roger Holder came to an abrupt end.

My arrangements for leaving Algiers were well advanced by that time. My biggest problem was not having a legitimate passport. The one I had left the States with, using the identity of my childhood friend, was very hot, so I needed a new solution.

After I had been in Algiers for about a year, I had been ordered by letter to surrender my false passport to the Swiss embassy, which was handling U.S.-Algeria relations following the Six-Day War, and the letter went on to cite the felony violation I had made in forging my identity. That meant the passport number was probably in the black book accessible to all customs agents in countries that were members of INTERPOL. I essentially no longer had a passport. I needed something cool if I was going to get back to the States safely.

Having read every book I could get my hands on dealing with intelligence and counterintelligence, hoping this knowledge would help me survive, I had learned that it was the Soviets who had best perfected the counterfeiting of American passports. From what I had read, their fakes couldn't be distinguished from the real thing. I decided to try to make contact and see if they would give me one. Cleaver had always condemned every so-called friendly government that never gave us any active support, but I also knew for a fact that none had ever been approached with a concrete request for anything. I hoped luck was on my side.

The Soviet Union embassy had a dedicated liaison for liberation movements, and I asked a comrade from an African liberation movement to work his connection with the man, officially a first secretary, to see if he could arrange a meeting between us at the Pointe. Both he and the first secretary agreed. After our introduction, it was time to make my move. I, as a representative of a militant movement, made my official request to the Soviet government for specific items of aid, and the first secretary agreed to forward my request to Moscow and promised to get back in touch when he received a reply.

After this meeting, the Soviets started sending invitations to the Panther office, asking us to attend all of their official functions. At a time when everyone else was dropping the Panthers from their guest lists, it was the Soviets who added us to theirs. They showed more courage toward us than anyone else. With the Panther split then being well known, and taking into account all the associated bad press that came with it, we were no longer desirable allies. Even the Algerians had dropped us, and everyone else had followed their lead—except the Soviets.

The comrade who had brought the first secretary to me and acted as our interpreter let me know that he could connect me with people who could get me a passport. He said passports were no problem. I had known that comrade ever since I had arrived in Algiers, but had never thought to broach the subject with him. I felt stupid, to say the least; a lot of precious time had been needlessly lost.

He put me in touch with the people who could help, and soon I had everything I needed to leave. It was only a matter of fixing a date. The American intelligence services were surely aware that we were all trying to leave Algiers, and it was all but certain that they were watching our movements closely in order to profit from any false moves and have us arrested and handed over to them if we strayed onto territory friendly to them. That had to be avoided at all cost.

The Soviet first secretary got back in touch then and said his government had agreed to everything. I was dumbfounded. The Soviets had said yes to all of my requests! All those years we had been condemning them for their revisionism, but at a time when everyone else was abandoning us, they came through. To show my appreciation, I led the first secretary to the wall where I had my maps hanging. I called his attention to what I considered my best one: a map that showed the location of all military installations inside the United States. When he recognized what it was, he became very interested and drew closer to inspect the date of publication. He was impressed when he saw it was only six months old. I also showed him my library of around fifty U.S. military manuals. He chose about a half dozen and asked if he could borrow them and the map for a few days. I had anticipated this request and was glad to say he could keep them as long as he liked. I then felt we were on equal footing. I always liked to pay my own way. When he returned everything a week later, he gave me a list of five manuals and asked if I could get them for him. I said I would see what I could do, but it would probably take two or three months. Two weeks later I had them. He was jubilant when I called him to come pick up the manuals.

In the meantime, I had gotten a passport from my other contact and was able to tell the first secretary that I would no longer need the things I had requested after all. I explained that I was in a hurry to move and that I appreciated his government's cooperation but I had to take the most rapid course. He understood, and to help me in my travels he gave me a thousand dollars and wished me good luck. Let history record that when we most needed solidarity, the Soviets came through. It was not a simple symbolic gesture; the dialectic can be found everywhere, in the most unusual places.

At last, I was ready to leave. Final arrangements were being made with the comrades who would be moving me, and if all went as planned, I would be gone before another month was out.

It was the end of July when news of another hijacking hit the airwaves. It was a flight from Detroit to Miami and sounded like the work of a group of blacks. They were in Miami waiting for a million-dollar ransom to be delivered along with a crew qualified to fly across the Atlantic. As they started the crossing, it was announced they were heading for Algiers. Obviously, it had to be people who didn't read newspapers or listen to the news; otherwise, they would have known that the ransom money would just be confiscated and given back to the U.S. government. As it turned out, they *had* heard that the Algerian government was going to give back the $500,000 that Roger had brought over, but they didn't believe it, thinking the news media was lying. Unfortunately for them, it was one time the media was telling the truth.

I telephoned the office and alerted everyone that another plane was on the way, and this time the hijackers were bringing $1 million. When I arrived at the office, everyone was already discussing how to divide up the money. Although they knew then that the initial $500,000 was going to be given back to the U.S. government, the actual transfer hadn't yet been carried out, and so now, with another million on the way, and with imaginations fueled by a desperate need for funds, it looked like everyone was again mistaking their dreams for reality. As soon as I understood the mood and what was going on, I announced that they could have my share. Pete O'Neal said, "Fine. Does anyone else feel that way?" I had to laugh. They were actually trying to think of some way to force President Boumédiène to give us the money. I warned them that if they made a move, the Algerians would move on them. I was convinced that the Algerians were not going to jeopardize the economic future of their country for $1.5 million and a handful of niggers. I was told I could keep my opinions to myself and was thanked for giving them my share of the money. With that, we all left for the airport.

When we got there, it was obvious that this time everything would be handled differently. As we approached the airport area, we found it was sealed off. We had to do some fast talking and fishing of cards to get through to the terminal, and then as soon as the security people saw us arrive, they kept us back in the passenger area. This time, it was serious business. I saw military trucks with rocket launchers on top. We could just barely see the tail of the plane, which had been directed to a remote corner of the tarmac. Now, I was not immune from dreaming myself, and I had decided that if I got the chance to get to the plane, I was going to explain to the hijackers the situation in Algiers, ask if I could join them, and then convince them to fly us all to a place where we might have a chance to hold on to the money. But that opportunity never came. We were kept far away from everything. I drove back to the Pointe and my radio.

At the office, they continued their desperate plans to get the money. They seemed to have lost all reason. Eldridge thought they might still have a chance if he could just speak to the hijackers, and he thought that chance might come when we were invited to a press conference featuring this new group of hijackers. The whole diplomatic corps was invited to attend, but as all the people invited started showing up, Algerian security turned everyone away. That was a surprise, but it didn't put so much as a dent in Eldridge's determination to get his hands on the money.

A few nights later, Cleaver came to the Pointe to give me a copy of a statement they had prepared and distributed to the International Press Corps. It was a heavy criticism of Algerian policies and Boumédiène, designed to pressure him into giving up the money. I was furious. I didn't agree with that at all. They had gone crazy. Plus, I hadn't been consulted. True, I was no longer part of the group, but the Algerian authorities didn't know that. They viewed all the Panthers in Algiers as a single entity, and I would be included in any consequences that resulted from the statement, and, for that reason alone, I should have been consulted or at least informed before the statement had been handed out. By the time Cleaver came to the Pointe, however, it was already on the wire. I was pissed off, to say the least.

At noon the next day, I heard news of the statement on the BBC. No more than a half hour passed before Larry called from the office to tell me it was surrounded by Algerian policemen with machine guns. He wanted me to call New York, quick, and get something going. I hung up the telephone, gathered all my weapons and ammunition and dope, and put everything in a suitcase, which I gave to my friend Andrea as I told her to get as far away from my house as she could. Then I called New York. As I was telling sister Bernice Jones what was going on, my doorbell started ringing at the same time someone started beating on the door. It was obvious who it was. Police all over the world act like you're deaf when they come on official business. They entered and proceeded to take the place apart. I had never witnessed such a thorough search. They left no stone unturned. The only thing they didn't search was the garbage. They found nothing, of course, and finally left.

Later, news accounts of the conflict between the Panthers and the Algerians made it clear why they had come. The Algerian authorities had made the mistake of telling the press they had moved on us for dope charges, and when that went out on the wire, they needed to put some action behind it. Since they knew we smoked hash and weed—because the people we bought it from were their own agents!—they never expected they wouldn't find any when they vamped on us. And they didn't even think to bring some to plant. If they could have treated everything as a criminal matter, they could have done what they wanted with us, but now that that had failed, they had, whether they liked it or not, a political problem on their hands. Everyone in the office was put under house arrest and the telephone was cut.

While Andrea and I were having dinner and discussing events, the doorbell rang. When I opened it, I saw plainclothes policemen parked all over the area. And the two cars right out front were full of blacks. They had brought all the hijackers to the Pointe and placed us all under house arrest. We could only go across the street, accompanied by a policeman, to buy groceries. They took Andrea and left.

Andrea had assisted us in many capacities since the fall of 1970, and among other things, she had occasionally acted as an interpreter and translator for us. Because of the impeccable French of the statement Eldridge had released to the press, the security people were convinced it was Andrea who had done the translation, and so they took her down to the station and tried to frighten her into signing a statement to the effect that we had administered drugs to her and she had been carried from the Pointe on a stretcher. She was threatened with twenty years in prison if she didn't sign, but she held out and, after being kept twenty-four hours, she was released. She had to leave the country and was not allowed back until two years later, after the last of the former Panthers had left.

All my plans for leaving were now blown. Not only was I stuck in my pad but my contact for leaving had disappeared. I hadn't been told who it was, so I couldn't even go looking for him. All those months of work down the drain. I was so stressed out, I had a terrible psychosomatic reaction. I awoke the next morning with my hands on fire. They itched like crazy, and no matter how much I scratched, I got no relief. I was miserable. After the house arrest was lifted a few days later, I went to the hospital, and when the doctor understood that I was a Panther, she gave me some tranquilizers and sent me home. Again, I knew I had to start from scratch and develop a new plan of departure.

There was one last thing I hadn't tried. I wrote a letter to President Boumédiène and the other Algerian officials, thanking them for the way they had related to our struggle and had provided us with their hospitality. I also wrote a press release making it clear that from that day forward I had severed all political relations with everyone and was no longer a member of the Black Panther Party, nor any other organization. That was the end.

Afterword

What did I hope to accomplish by writing this memoir? When my seventeen-year-old son, Donnie, asked me to tell him everything that had happened to me, the only way I could think of effectively doing that was by writing it down. That was the immediate catalyst. But the belief that this history needed to be told has been simmering on the back burner for some time now.

Because of the accident of my birth, both in terms of social conditions and geographic location, my consciousness and commitment to the struggle developed in the context of the unyielding quest for freedom and justice for black people in the United States. As I write this in the beginning of 1981 and examine the conditions of black people from my view in exile, I see that, objectively, conditions are worse now than they were when I was first pushed by some inner force to become active in trying to improve them.

The gap between the average income of blacks and whites has widened. There are far more blacks unemployed today than there were in 1967, when I joined the Black Panther Party. Moves are on all across the country to cut back or eliminate social programs designed to "improve" the conditions of blacks. And the government is making moves toward legislation that would take away the gains of the civil rights movement of the fifties and sixties. The specter of terrorism and violence directed toward blacks has found a second wind and is sweeping the country.

The nation's capitalist system is in a stage of crisis, in part because former colonies that were the sources of unlimited riches in the form of raw materials have since gained their political independence, and some have now begun the process of attaining their economic independence as well, simply by charging fairer prices for their valuable resources. I believe the capitalist system as we know it has passed its historic summit and is now faced with the reality of decline. Make no mistake about it, capitalism is still powerful and has a lot of fight left, but the maintenance of capitalism is still dependent upon the creation of new capital. As the worldwide competition for resources and markets reaches its equilibrium—there's no place else to go, as the world is all divided up—the only solution left in this never-ending quest for capital is to turn the screws tighter at home.

This phenomenon is not confined to the United States. It's the same all over the world. The present economic crisis is going to continue and get worse—not in a straight line, but with ups and downs. Nevertheless, viewed in historical terms, it is, and will continue to be, a decline.

The basis of the world's social problems is economic. Everyone has to eat, sleep, and shelter themselves from the environment, yet xenophobia, often manifesting as discrimination based on race, ethnicity, and religion, has historically controlled who has access to these basic needs. Castes are created and maintained within the class system, and in the present economic order of things, only the crumbs are distributed to those in the lower classes, again as defined by skin color, ethnic origin, and religious beliefs. Inside the United States, it's whites against blacks. In Northern Ireland, it's Catholics against Protestants. In Chad, it's tribe against tribe.

To understand the deteriorating conditions inside the United

States, we have to be aware of this context. Blacks are still the last hired and first fired, and that's not going to change, but now the dominant culture must find new ways to work within the current system. For some, it has been profitable to cede certain "civil rights" and say okay, come on in, the door's open. Billions of dollars have been made marketing black American culture, and the result is that demands of a nationalist nature are met while, at the same time, those who have learned to harness that market are making a profit. I remember when Melvin Van Peebles made the film *Sweet Sweetback's Baadasssss Song,* in 1971. Suddenly, the system saw the economic potential of the black movie audience and there was a mad rush to start cranking out "black films."

With the sudden exposure of blacks everywhere, but mainly in the visible areas of culture and politics, many people, both black and white, and both inside and outside the United States, got the impression that progress was being made. But that's to ignore much of the bigger picture. It's true that Nixon was a crook, but he was a slick crook, and his administration was effective in creating a new class of nigger, one that had never existed before. His niggers were violent, drug-pushing criminals, and they were very visible and vocal, giving the impression that they were the majority. In reality this was a very small number of people, but the public didn't know any better. While that smokescreen was being spread around the globe, black people were more or less lulled into the trap of believing the only way to survive was "every man for himself." Everyone got tricked into thinking that if they didn't make it, it was their own fault, regardless of what systems of oppression had kept them down.

And now? The unemployed/underemployed and uneducated/undereducated poor are using the only means they know of to deal with their daily survival, and they are widely punished for it. Prisons across the country are being filled with black youth. The prison population in New York State is almost 50 percent black, although blacks make up only 14 percent of the population. Those are the official statistics, and they are mirrored in community after community. What will happen as more become unemployed and unemployable?

I don't consider the force that pushed me to become active as a militant as anything unique. Therefore, I don't consider it wishful thinking on my part to expect that, sooner or later, others will organize themselves to try to change the existing conditions. Those of us with experiences in the struggle have a historical responsibility to pass them on; otherwise, every time a new formation comes along, they will be starting from scratch, just as we did. Mistakes are the nursery of new ideas, so we must share them too; if we continue to hide and distort our errors, those coming after us will be condemned to repeat them. We cannot afford the luxury of leaving it up to historians to reveal what we did after fifty or one hundred years have passed. Present conditions demand we tell our stories now. We also have a responsibility to those who died in the struggle, or were imprisoned, or were forced into exile to escape those fates.

The deaths of Fred Bennett, Robert "Spider" Webb, William Seidler, Rahim (Clinton Robert Smith), and Sam Napier should not be swept under the rug. Each of these martyrs were, in their own way, active participants in the struggle for freedom and justice. The circumstances of their deaths are no reason to bury them in silence. We must dissect and analyze the reasons for their deaths so we can learn how to avoid such tragedies in the future.

It is imperative that we add social psychology to our analytical toolkit, and all the natural sciences, too. Any strategies—any plans for the future of our species that don't take into account the biological, evolutionary nature of mankind—are doomed to a checkmate.

The major weakness—one that inevitably leads to failure—is Lenin's idea that a party should be structured according to the tenets of democratic centralism. Under utopian conditions, with everyone being more or less an angel, it would probably work; but given our present stage of evolutionary development, with all our human strengths and weaknesses, it is just not possible to pull it off. Lenin either gave no consideration to or ignored the fact that whenever a member of the human species gets into a position to exercise power something goes haywire. Since all intellectual activity is subjective, those exercising power—defined as the ability to use resources, whether human or otherwise, to act upon the environment to bring about change—do so in their own subjective ways. The degree of benefit to the masses is dependent upon the coincidence of the subjective ideas of those exercising power and the real needs of the people.

Given the present state of our social development, in which power is often centered on small groups, we must be extremely vigilant. Progressive organizations that presume to move in the interest of the masses must constantly confront the psychology of power. In some form or fashion, they must devise checks and balances to control the madness that seems to arise whenever power is concentrated in the hands of a few individuals. Democratic centralism is not the answer. It is the mechanism that gave us Stalin and Hilliard. Inevitably, when this form of organizational structure is adopted, centralism is emphasized, often to the detriment of democracy, and that leads to authoritarianism, to bureaucracy, and to dictatorship.

The paradox in what I believe and say lies in the fact that I see no other way to consciously change economic and social conditions without some form of organization. And organization means structure, and structure means hierarchy. Or maybe I'm wrong. Perhaps it can be done another way. But, as a hypothesis, I would say that an organization is a prerequisite for bringing about economic and social change on a national level, and that means individuals will inevitably rise to positions of power. The challenge is to find a way for an organization to effectively deal with the problems of change and yet not deteriorate into a tool for individuals to amass personal power. We have to prevent those exercising power from becoming new versions of Hitler, Stalin, Pinochet, Franco, Somoza, Papa and Baby Doc, Idi Amin, Bokassa, Joe McCarthy, J. Edgar Hoover, Nixon, and, to bring it on home, Huey Newton and Eldridge Cleaver. How did it happen?

As far as I was concerned, it was their ability to inspire admiration and the desire to emulate them, coupled with their wish to take the strongest stand against the problems of injustice. In relating to the most powerful Panthers as "leaders," I wanted to do whatever they wanted me to do. I gave no consideration to seeing them, let alone understanding them, as flawed human beings, as just people. I never searched for, or even considered the possibility of, hidden motivations behind their moves or decisions. I and so many others made no analysis, just followed with blind faith. Some might be amazed at such a confession of naïveté, especially in this day and age. I put that on my rural religious upbringing, the weight of which I will carry to my grave.

But there can be no leader without a group of followers, and so we must take some blame. I submit my personal history as a case study. And yet the problem is far deeper than anything I have exposed. It seems that at our present level of evolutionary development as a species, we are constantly in search of a messiah—a messiah to help us deal with the burden of the struggle for our everyday survival. When Huey and Eldridge manifested themselves, they were, for many of us, the messiahs. The very nature of the campaign to free Huey, as conceived by Cleaver, was in fact the creation of a cult of personality. Newton became our god. On all subjects on which he felt the need to express himself, he became the sole possessor of truth. His every word became the law and line of the party.

After Newton's imprisonment and Cleaver's exile, we began to study Marxism-Leninism to arm ourselves with an analytical tool to help us deal with the situation we were confronted with. At that point, it was David Hilliard who exhibited the most skillful capacity for articulating and manipulating the new language we were learning. He was chief of staff and the highest-ranking member of the central committee, and also free and available to make decisions on a day-to-day basis. The combination of those factors, plus the party structure of so-called democratic centralism, but in which only the centralism part was ever implemented, plus Hilliard's infatuation with Stalin, plus Newton's support of this order of things upon his release, created the malignant combination that led to the destruction of the Black Panther Party.

I do not agree with the widespread idea that it was the repression by law enforcement agencies that destroyed the Black Panther Party. Of course, they did much harm. But each blatant act of repression was accompanied by growing support among the people. The public repression the party received was clear evidence, for all to see, that the things we were saying about the repressive, exploitative nature of the American system were true. And after the murder of Fred Hampton in his bed as he slept, even our staunchest detractors began giving consideration to what we had been saying.

We refuse our own history by blaming every negative thing

that occurred on the COINTELPRO. That is a very convenient way of avoiding analysis. That also gives the pigs much more credit than they merit.

When Huey fell, we so desperately wanted to save him from their clutches, and possibly the gas chamber, that we glorified him—far and wide, north and south, east and west. The *actual* Huey could not survive the Huey that we had created.

How many could have resisted? We killed Huey with our love!

Inevitably, in searching for causes of the failure of the Black Panther Party, I end up focusing on its internal contradictions and the relationship between the leaders and the led. One thing is certain: neither Newton nor Cleaver nor Hilliard could have done anything alone; every historical sociopolitical criminal had to have followers at one time or another. As we go forward, we must remember that we, both as individuals and as a collective mass, in our desperate search for guidance in our daily struggle for survival, have historically had the tendency to follow, blindly, the first person that comes along who seems to be effectively dealing with what we consider our immediate survival problems. The study of world history, or of the twentieth century alone, shows repeatedly the disasters wrought by this tendency. The tragedy of mass suicide at Jim Jones's Peoples Temple in Guyana in 1978 is one recent example.

Another malignant force in the party's decline was the relationships between the "sisters" and "brothers." Many excellent militants were forced from the party because they refused to submit to the violation of their free choice, which included interpersonal relations. Over time, it became so elementary and simplistic: if a sister didn't give in to the sexual demands of a brother, she was considered counterrevolutionary. In terms of the party platform, we were making great strides in advancing the cause of equality of the sexes, and all ground-level work was done on an equal basis, without regard to sex, but then when it came to deciding strategy and political direction, women were nowhere to be found. And when it came to choosing a sexual partner, sisters were expected to submit to the demands of the men, with no free choice in the matter. That was a phenomenon I saw originate and develop at headquarters, and it soon spread to other branches of the party, always in the wake of visits from the leaders. After Huey was released, I heard there were virtual orgies. I'm sure I missed more than I saw. I'm eager to read the history of the Black Panther Party as written by a sister.

Now I feel the need to address the question of armed struggle, especially given my past activities. I consider any discussions or arguments for or against armed struggle as dealing with a false problem, one that doesn't get to the root of the larger situation. History shows there is not one instance when a group that led or ruled another group gave up their privileges peacefully. Whenever the masses demand a more equitable distribution for the benefit of society, the exact opposite occurs. The minority in power (the rulers) inevitably use whatever force necessary to maintain and guarantee their privileges and status. If the subjective conditions are ripe and the struggle cannot be checked, the result is often war. History seems to indicate there cannot be a fundamental change in social and economic relationships without some form of armed struggle.

Armed struggle always follows the use of so-called legal forms of struggle, and then it is only successful in bringing about the desired economic and social changes when it is accompanied by a critical mass of people feeling a desire, determination, and will to sacrifice—even their lives—to the cause. Whenever small groups engage in armed struggle that the majority of people are not ready to go along with, support, or join in such efforts, they suffer the same fate as the Baadar-Meinhof group in Germany, who ended up defeated and isolated. Courage, determination, and combativeness of isolated groups is just not enough. As far as I am concerned, armed struggle is the midwife that delivers the new society that has been carried in the womb of the old, but it has to have widespread support.

As it plays out in the United States, I think that even though the objective conditions are favorable, the subjective conditions are such that the time has not yet come to begin the war for change. Much work has to be done before that day arrives. Most people have to be convinced that there is no other alternative for real, meaningful, fundamental changes in economic and social conditions. Then, the question is not whether one is for or against armed struggle; it is a question of understanding dynamic forces and knowing when to initiate armed struggle for maximum effect.

Every generation produces its warriors—courageous, strong, and impatient. I have a suggestion for those individuals in the United States who don't want to consider anything other than armed actions. To them I say there is plenty to do in constituting groups to deal with the defense of the community, although the form that should take has to be determined by the specific conditions wherever you are. It is significant to note that for the last twenty years, the only time there was a significant decrease in terrorism and violence directed against the black community was when there were groups organized militarily who were active in resistance to such violence. I believe there is always a place for defensive actions. Today, I am convinced that whenever a policeman, or any other, kills a black person, if the consequence was that the specific murderer were then himself executed, that would bring about a decrease in the terrorism and violence now directed toward the black community. The creation of the necessary machinery to do that is more than enough to occupy those who feel the need to move in a military manner at the present time. Time and energy used arguing for or against armed struggle would be more productive if it were used to figure out what steps could be taken, at the present time, to bring about collective consciousness and the understanding of real problems.

It is also wise to acknowledge the fact that it is Congress who has the power to make or change laws that govern the functioning of the country. It seems reasonable—and something a majority of people could support—to consider the creation of another political party that would be a real alternative to the two-ring circus of the Democrats and the Republicans. They are only two different masks hiding the same faces of those who have the real power today. The new party would be one whose strategy and tactics would be directed toward solving the day-to-day and long-term social and economic problems of the majority of people. It would have to be structured in such a way that dogmas and sectarianism would be excluded, and no effort should be ignored to make it understood by all that, behind the smokescreen of racial distinctions, the basic problems are the same for everyone: we all need food, clothing, and shelter. It would be interesting to see what changes could be brought about by such a party if it were successful in organizing and mobilizing enough support to elect a majority to Congress. Of course it would have to be enough of a majority to override presidential vetoes. And of course, I'm just dreaming. Yet what is tomorrow made of but dreams?

Acknowledgments

John Keker, thank you so much for stepping in when my Daddy couldn't. It meant the world to my family.

Maureen Stone, you called me your ride-or-die chick. It goes both ways. Love you always.

Liz Hasse and Steve Wasserman, thank you so much for being more than an attorney and a publisher: thanks for being friends.

To "the cousins": Jan Griffin, Allison Griffin, Billye Sutton, Robert "Bobby" Young, and Michelle Neely. Whenever I needed pictures or information, I could always count on you. Love you guys!

—Kimberly Cox Marshall

About the Author

Born in Missouri in 1936, Donald L. Cox joined the Black Panther Party in 1967, one year after its founding. Appointed as the party's field marshal and known as "DC," he was soon inducted into the party's high command as a member of its central committee, and he founded the party's San Francisco office. In 1970, he fled the United States and helped open the party's International Section in Algiers. Two years later, he resigned from the party and left Algeria. Except for a brief trip when he entered and exited the United States incognito using a false passport, he lived in France, supporting himself as a professional house painter and freelance photographer. He also worked to create a computer database about the history of African American revolutionary movements. Ultimately he earned enough cash to buy and renovate a small mountain redoubt in the village of Camps-sur-l'Agly, where he died at age seventy-four in February 2011.

A Note on Type

Marion is an original transitional serif typeface. It has some aspects of Century Schoolbook, softened by a little Baskerville flavor. Angled elliptical ball terminals gently suggest a nib angle while clawhammer shapes give the *c*, *g*, and *s* a somewhat aggressive personality.

This typeface has three styles and was designed by Ray Larabie and published by Typodermic Fonts Inc.